Darkness Hides the Flowers

A TRUE STORY OF HOLOCAUST SURVIVAL

BY JERRY L. JENNINGS
AS TOLD BY IDA HOFFMANN FIRESTONE

Print information available on the last page.

Book Designer: Jerome Cuyos

To order additional copies of this book, contact:
Xlibris
1-888-795-4274
www.Xlibris.com
Orders@Xlibris.com

Darkness Hides the Flowers

A TRUE STORY OF HOLOCAUST SURVIVAL

TABLE OF CONTENTS

Note: Cover painting by Ida Hoffmann Firestone, depicting a French farm that briefly sheltered her during her flight from the Nazis.

Painting of her father by Ida Hoffmann Firestone.

Ida Hoffmann Firestone dedicates this book
to the memory of her beloved parents,
Adolphe and Berthe Hoffmann,
and to her son,
Craig Joseph Firestone.

CONTACT INFORMATION:
jerryj100@comcast.net

Title Poem: Darkness Hides the Flowers

DARKNESS HIDES THE FLOWERS	L'OBSCURITÉ CACHE LES FLEURS
Lying on the straw mat	Sur la paille, allongée je suis
I will spend the day and the night	J'y passerai la journée et la nuit
I continue to be afraid	Peureuse, je continue d'être
I see people through the gaps in the wall	Des fentes du mur, les gens je guette
Tomorrow I will leave	Demain je partirai
At the next village	Au prochain village
I will find a house	Une maison je trouverai
To think about it, gives me	D'y penser me donne
The courage to go on	Le courage de continuer
I must force myself to walk	Me forcer a marcher je dois
I see the rooftops of houses	Les toits des maisons, je vois
The clouds are starting to form	Les nuages commencent a se former
I must protect myself from the rain	De la pluie, je me protegerai
I am cold, I shiver, I am hungry	J'ai froid, je frissonne, j'ai faim
Oh! To find a piece of bread	Oh! De trouver un morceau de pain
The darkness hides the flowers	L'obscurité cache les fleurs
They have lost their colors	Ells ont perdu leur couleur
Tomorrow morning, I will rejoice	Demain matin, je me rejouirai
To have found them again	De les avòir retrouvées

Written by Ida Hoffmann Firestone in August 1944 while hiding from the Gestapo.

CHAPTER ONE

The Scar-Faced Man

I was playing outside that day. I was alone and I knew to stay close to home. But it was France in May and the flowers were being pulled open by the midday sun, just like I was being pulled outside by the same radiance. It was a perfect day for a girl of thirteen. I felt like a song, standing by the door to our apartment house, watching the people passing by. *"Bon jour Madame." "Bon jour Monsieur."*

Then a grim man in his 50's abruptly appeared — and the song in my chest stopped. I knew he was German by his long black trench coat and green fedora with a feather. He marched past me as if I was invisible and entered my building. I suddenly felt cold, as if the sun had been extinguished, and wondered why the German had come — and whether he had come for my family.

After waiting two minutes, I had to know. I followed after him, climbing the stairs that led to our second floor apartment. As I climbed the stairs, I could already hear my mother crying loudly. "Please, please don't kill my husband," *Maman* wailed, "please don't kill my husband."

Without breathing, I stepped inside our apartment and stood by the door. My mother was standing before the German, begging him for mercy. His arrogance was as hideous as the scar stretching from the right corner of his nose to his jaw line. Seeing me, my mother said, "Sit." Her voice was hushed, her eyes pained. She wanted me to run away, but she couldn't say so. So I sat at the dining room table, where my oldest sister Rosa was already sitting.

My mother offered a seat to the scar-faced man. He scowled at the chair — with its grapes and leaves embossed in leather on the back and on the seat — and spat on it. "Pteu!" Instinctively, *Maman* went to wipe the chair, but the scar-faced man sat on his own spit. He declared that he had come from the Gestapo to arrest my father — because someone had denounced him as a Communist — not because he was Jewish. "We know your husband is a collaborator because he came from Russia," he sneered.

"Yes, my husband was originally from Russia," my mother pleaded, "but he left to escape from the Communists. My husband was never a Communist." The scar-faced man was unfazed. *Maman* continued to beg him not to kill my father, insisting that he had never been a Communist. But the Gestapo man just sat there, stone-faced, encased in his black leather coat.

"Would you like some music?" *Maman* tried to think of anything to please him. "My daughter will play for you. What would you like? Ida will play something for you."

The scar on his face twisted slightly as he yielded to my mother's invitation and grunted his permission.

Maman looked to me and I rose to go to the piano. My legs were shaking. My hands were shaking. What could I play? How could I play? My quivering fingers could hardly turn the pages of my piano music. My first thought was to play *My Yiddishe Mama*. It was one of my favorites and I knew it by heart, but then I realized, "Oh no, never that!"

Since he was German, I figured I should play something German. I turned the pages of my sheet music to find *Blue Danube*. It is a long Strauss piece, but fortunately, I knew it well. I sobbed as I played the Strauss as faithfully as possible. Tears of fright poured down my cheeks and I could hear the intermittent whispers of my mother, still begging the scar-faced man, "Please don't kill my husband..." I glanced over my shoulder – just once – to see *Maman* on her knees, kissing his black shoes. Somehow I continued to play.

Finally, the Gestapo man stood up. He said only, "I'll be back," and marched out.

I stopped playing the piano as soon as he was gone. *Maman* instantly collapsed. Rosa and *Maman* cried and cried. I felt immense relief. The beast had put his teeth to our throats, but he had not bitten.

Our thoughts turned to Papa. He was a machinist at the iron foundry in Pont-a-Mousson, which had rotating shifts of 5 am to 1 pm, 1 pm to 9 pm, and 9 pm to 5 am. Today Papa was working the second shift. It would be many hours before we would hear the clatter of father bringing his bicycle into the downstairs hallway and propping it in the corner. We sat for hours, waiting, waiting, waiting. Meanwhile, my second oldest sister, Eugenie, and my little brother, Arnold, had returned home.

"If you want dinner, I'll make you dinner," *Maman* said. "But if you want to wait for Papa to come home, then we'll wait and eat together."

We had no appetite. "We'll wait."

Finally, after 9 pm, Papa came home. Of course, he knew nothing of what had happened. When we told him, he tried to conceal his fear, but his face was white and distorted.

"Don't worry, he's not going to come back," my mother concluded.

Papa looked at her in surprise. "How do you know? Did he tell you?"

"No," she replied with a peculiar confidence, "But he is a coward, so he won't come back."

My father considered her words, then shook his head. "None of them are cowards. They are all killers." There was fear on his face, but also rage – rage that this awful scar-faced man had just terrorized our family and he was helpless to protect us.

I slept soundly that night – from the exhaustion of having been so terrified.

The next day my father went back to work – as if it was a normal day for any foundry worker. And we children went back to school – as if it was a normal day for any French child in Pont-a-Mousson in 1942.

CHAPTER TWO

Life in Pont-a-Mousson

Pont-a-Mousson is a lovely little city, divided by the River Moselle. I had lived there all my life. My family's home was on the west side, *Saint Laurent*, which had about 30,000 people. The east side, *Saint Martin*, was smaller. Wherever you look, the city is pretty and elegant, a colorful place cradled between wooded hills so picturesque that, decades later, I painted them from memory. I knew every street and store. Even today, nearly sixty years since I left Pont-a-Mousson, I could take you on any street and know exactly where we are.

In the center of the city is a large "town square" called *Place Duroc*, which is actually shaped like a giant equilateral triangle. It is lined with arcaded houses from the sixteenth to eighteenth centuries. On Saturdays, the local people would go to the *Place Saint Antoine*, just a few blocks away, and fill the open area with tables to display their wares. Farmers from the surrounding area would sell fresh produce. Merchants and common folk would sell all sorts of products, crafts and French delicacies. In the summertime, there would be carnivals and fairs with rides, games, candy and ice cream.

Place Duroc, the triangle, was the true heart of Pont-a-Mousson. One corner of the triangle points to a bridge that connects the two sides of the city. From *Place Duroc*, you can see all the way through the town to the tall cathedral of *Eglise Saint Martin* on the other side of the river. The *Abbaye des Prémontrés*, a magnificent abbey from the 18th century, also stands on the river bank on the *Saint Martin* side. The cathedral and the Abbey symbolize the proud, deeply Catholic character of Pont-a-Mousson.

Outside the city, the remains of an ancient castle stand on top of a steep hill called *La Colline de Mousson* (the Hill of Mousson). *La Colline* was a favorite outing for hiking and picnics, offering a beautiful view of the countryside from the castle's broken stone walls, still standing twenty feet high.

Pont-a-Mousson is 150 miles due east of Paris in the northeastern region of France known as "Meurthe/Moselle." This rural area is marked by its vast forests, rugged hills and isolated farms and villages. Located midway between the busy cities of Metz, eighteen miles to the north, and Nancy, nineteen miles to the south, Pont-a-Mousson is a crossroads of sorts — and it was of strategic importance in three successive wars between France and Germany: the Franco-Prussian War in 1870, the First World War in 1914, and, in my time, the Second World War in 1940 and again in 1944.

*   *   *

Painting of Pont-a-Mousson by Ida Hoffmann Firestone.

My parents first moved to Pont-a-Mousson in 1925. They were both born in the Ukraine, which was part of Russia at that time. My father, Adolphe Goffmann, was three years older than my mother, Berthe Blanc, who was sometimes called "Bella." My mother came from Odessa, a large city located on the Black Sea in the southern Ukraine. My father came a town called Ghitomir, which is near Kiev in the northern Ukraine. I know very little about my family history except that my father's father was an architect and that my father was a Russian soldier when he met my mother. My mother had been hospitalized during a typhoid epidemic and my father had volunteered with some other young soldiers to help at the local hospital. They fell in love during her stay.

Adolphe Hoffmann in a German transit camp in 1925.
Painting by Ida Hoffmann Firestone.

In October 1917, the Bolshevik Revolution shook Russia and the world. Though my father was not politically involved, he needed to escape from the Communists in 1920. So my parents fled on foot through the thick forests to reach safety in Estonia. From Estonia, they moved on to Germany in search of work.

When the German immigration authorities asked my father his name, he said "Goffmann."

They replied, "No, here in Germany the name is Hoffmann," and immediately changed it. For this reason, our family name was changed from a clearly Jewish name to a German name.

At first, the German authorities put my parents in some kind of transit camp. I painted this portrait of my father from a photograph that was taken while he was in the transit camp in Germany in 1925 at the age of 35. His clothes were battered and torn.

Adolphe Hoffmann and Berthe Blanc
as a young couple (about 1924).

My parents tried to live in Berlin for three and half years, but the German economy was in ruin and my father could not find work. They also struggled to start a family. My mother had given birth to three boys – one in Russia, one in Estonia, and another in Germany – and each baby boy died in his infancy. Fortunately, the fourth child, my oldest sister Rosa, was a healthy child born in Berlin.

In 1925, my father learned of a possible job at an iron foundry in Pont-a-Mousson, France. He quickly decided to move there. Eventually he became a machinist in charge of the turbines at the Blenod factory, which we called "the foundry." It was one of two iron foundries in Pont-a-Mousson. His final employment papers from the *Societe de Fonderies de Pont-a-Mousson* indicate that Papa was "a machinist in the electric station."

My father came to France without knowing any French. But he was a brilliant man and had the knack for learning languages quickly. He could speak eight languages: Russian, Polish, Yiddish, Czech, Hungarian, and German – and later, French and English.

Ida's parents, Adolphe and Berthe Hoffmann, walking under the arcade of
Place Duroc in Pont-a-Mousson with Rosa and Eugenie (about 1926).

My mother then followed Papa to Pont-a-Mousson, bringing my sister Rosa, who had been born in Berlin and was now six months old. One year later, in 1926, my sister Eugenie was born in Pont-a-Mousson.

Then, in February 1929, my mother gave birth to me in our apartment on the second floor of #25 *Rue des Fosses*. My earliest memory is of marching with my sisters. In the kitchen, there was a cabinet near the stove where my mother kept the cooking utensils. My older sisters Rosa and Eugenie and I would take out three long wooden spoons, hold them high, and march around the table, chanting and singing.

A woman named Madame Manor lived downstairs. She adored me and was always kissing me. She called me, "*Salope.*" It is a bad word actually, meaning a slovenly, sluttish woman, but she used it as a pet name for me, a term of endearment. I was too little to pronounce it. I could only say, "'*lope*" instead of *Salope* and "patam" instead of *Madame*. So we girls marched around the kitchen table, spoons raised, chanting, "*Lope patam Manor! Lope patam Manor!*"

One day, my father surprised us by bringing home a goat! He put it in the yard in the back. For several days, we watched the goat from the window, while Papa fattened her up with food. We wanted to play with the goat, but Papa warned us that we might get hurt. "Don't get too fond of her," he said, "she's only here for a short visit." I was too young to grasp what would happen to the goat. We ate the goat meat. Trust me, today I would never touch it.

The incident with the goat was very unusual, but it shows how seriously my father took his role as the provider and protector of the family. In particular, he always made sure that we had fresh fruit in our home. Not just a bag or two. Papa would bring home entire crates of fruit. We were free to walk over and enjoy a piece of fruit anytime we pleased. He had very strong convictions about eating healthy food. For the same reason, Papa frowned on cakes and sweets. We almost never had cake in our home, which is probably why I love cake so much today. I could eat it every day.

My family later moved downstairs to the first floor apartment at *Rue des Fosses*, where my little brother Arnold was born. The apartment was a bit bigger. A few years later, when I was seven years old, my family moved again to an apartment at 1 *Rue Charles Lepois* in Pont-a-Mousson. This apartment was more spacious and comfortable. I remember how we would open a black metal door that entered into a garden. We would cross the little garden to climb up to our second floor apartment. By this time my brother Arnold, was a toddler. After losing four infant boys to early death, including one who was born after me, *Maman* had herself a healthy boy at last – and she adored him.

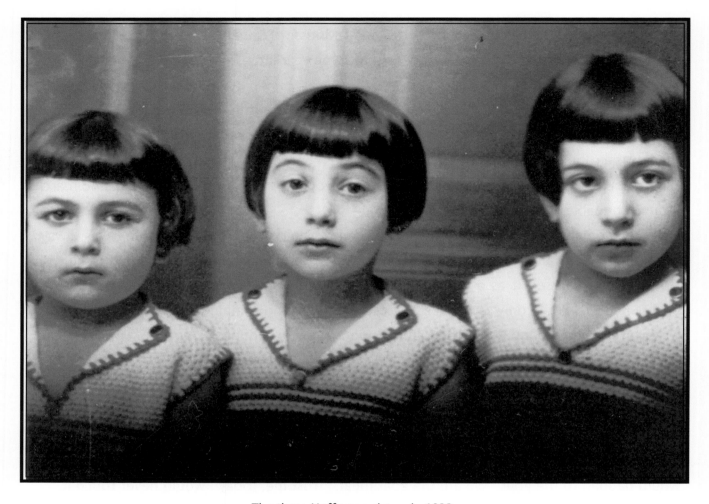

The three Hoffmann sisters in 1932:
from the left to right, Ida (age 3), Eugenie and Rosa.

Now there were four children in our family: Rosa, Eugenie, Ida (me) and Arnold. We were all polite and well-behaved – but not because we were afraid of punishment, for we were rarely spanked. We learned from example. It simply was the way we lived. My father would always say, "*Il faut toujours être une Dame.*" "You should always be a lady." This was our guiding rule. "If someone says something that you don't like or that makes you angry, don't say anything back." I never did. I never answered back – maybe to a fault. It was not until a few years ago that I spoke up for the first time in my life. Someone hurt me deeply and I said to myself, "All my life, I have allowed people to step on me, insult me, do things to hurt me. Now it is time for me to defend myself." So I did – and it felt great!

Papa also emphasized education. "Without education, you cannot do anything in life." He knew this from his own experience. Papa could have achieved more than being a machinist in an iron foundry. But the Russian Revolution and political exile ended his only chance of getting a university education. Still, Papa was very smart and artistic. Though untrained in art, Papa could draw marvelous pictures, especially birds, and sometimes he would paint. Most of all, he loved Russian poetry. People were amazed at how he could recite Russian poetry from

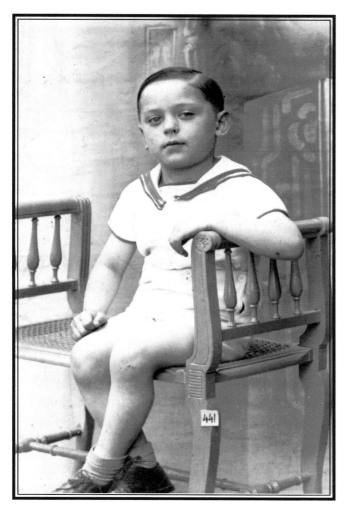 

The four Hoffmann children from left to right, youngest to oldest:
Arnold, Ida, Eugenie and Rosa.

memory for hours – and with great passion! Sometimes we would sit and listen as he recited poems in Russian. Although we were young children and did not understand a word of Russian, we could feel his passion and knew that this was something precious and magnificent.

As a family, we were close. We spent all of our time together – mostly because my parents were immigrant Jews and they were very few Jews in Pont-a-Mousson. We had no relatives within a thousand miles. The other relatives had moved to America before the Russian Revolution, when people were still free to emigrate. My father had a brother and a sister in Philadelphia. My mother had one brother in Cleveland and another in Columbus, Ohio, who had four children. One daughter went into show business under the name "Rose Blane." I never met her, but she would have been my first cousin. Rose Blane was the featured singer for a popular band called the Abe Lyman Orchestra. She married the conductor and they lived in Hollywood. In 1945, Rose Blane had a hit song with the Abe Lyman Orchestra called *Rum and Coca Cola*, which was also covered by the Andrews Sisters.

The Jewish community in Pont-a-Mousson was very small, maybe ten families altogether, but it was not close. We knew every Jewish person by name and face, but we did not socialize. Some would not even acknowledge that they knew us. I think that a few felt they were superior to us because my father worked in the iron foundry. One Jewish family had a female doctor. One family owned a butcher shop, though it was not a kosher one. Another sold fruit as a business. Another owned and operated a metal salvage business, and they employed a man from another Jewish family.

There was a single tiny synagogue in Pont-a-Mousson with a part-time Rabbi. The Rabbi owned a car and made his living by peddling underwear from village to village. It was a pretty synagogue, with men downstairs and women upstairs, separated in the Orthodox manner. There were two double doors on *Rue Charles Lepois,* which led to a courtyard, and then you would find the synagogue beyond. As a child, I wondered why the synagogue was so hidden. My feeling was that it was because of anti-Semitism. We did not go to synagogue very often and we were not very religious at home, but we had a strong family pride in being Jewish. Even as a small child, I thought of myself as Jewish first, then French.

When we were young, we rarely played outside. Not because the town was unsafe, but *Maman* was very protective. My older sisters, Rosa and Eugenie, were closer in age, so they spent more time with each other. I would usually play with my little brother, even though he was five years younger. Arnold was happy to play with me. We would lay the kitchen chair on the floor and make believe that it was a horse-drawn carriage. Arnold would be the milkman and I would sell the milk, or Arnold would be a peddler, and I would sell the goods. Occasionally, we would all play together. I remember a time when we again took my mother's three big wooden spoons and marched around the table, spoons held high, singing, *"On vient, on vient merci. Merci on vient,"* which means "here we come." It was my idea for us to sing.

We were a middle class family. Papa made a good salary as a machinist at the iron foundry. Papa did not trust banks so my little brother's mattress served as the bank. *Maman* was a homemaker. She would go to a dress-maker to have clothes made for us. Though we all received new clothes, I often wore hand-me-downs from my older sisters. When a coat or dress became too tight on my sister, it would be passed down to me. I wore one coat, in particular, for many years. It was Navy blue with four big buttons. Every few years, as I grew bigger, the tailor would expand the coat to fit me. Even after the war ended, I still wore that coat.

My mother was an angel, patient and kind. Her primary concern was to take care of the family, keep our home clean, and feed us well. She was an excellent cook. Nearly every Thursday, *Maman* would take us out into the fresh air for a long walk along the *Boulevard de Riolles*, which we simply called "The Boulevard." In Europe in those days, we went to school on Saturday rather than Thursday.

School and education were supremely important in our family. I attended kindergarten at the *Ecole Maternelle* and then I went to *Ecole Saint Jean* for elementary school. In France, everyone attended school until age 11 or 12, then each student would have to pass a national examination to graduate. If you passed, you were qualified to advance to high school. If you failed, you would go to a trade school to learn a vocation. At first, I attended the public high school for girls called *Ecole Superieure*. However, in 1941, the school was bombed and destroyed. The girls were then mixed into the high school for boys called *le College de Pont-a-Mousson*. We called it, "*le College*" for short.

I was a good student. As soon as we came home from school, we did our homework. We could not go out to play until our duty was done. I loved Math, but I was dreadful in art. When one teacher saw my drawings, he would say, "God in heaven, who sent you here?!" I was that bad at drawing. It's funny, but I simply cannot draw. I paint. When I paint, I immediately paint my subject – and it's lovely. But if someone had asked me then, I would have said that I had no artistic ability at all. The same was true for poetry. For me, it must come directly from my soul like painting. When I was little, I tried to write a few poems. But I did not like them and tore them up. Later, during the war, poetry became my savior.

School was also the place where we encountered the most anti-Semitism. The other children would often call us, "*sale Juive*" – "dirty Jew." Overt anti-Semitic remarks were rare among our close neighbors, but common at school and even for some adults and teachers. One time my mother was extremely upset because a particular girl was constantly calling me a "dirty Jew." So we went to the girl's house. I was standing next to my mother outside the door as *Maman* complained to the girl's mother – obviously without effect. So *Maman* tried a different tact: "Did you know that your Jesus was Jewish?" The woman responded by slamming the door in our faces.

I remember asking my mother, "Why do the Christians treat us this way?" Papa interceded before she could answer. "I'll tell her," he declared. Then he sat up straight and important like the President. "Do you know why they act like that? They are jealous of us. Because Jews are very smart, and we are very talented, and our women behave like ladies, and our men behave like gentlemen. That's why."

Later, I wondered about Papa's explanation. I knew there were girls in my school, who were also very smart and talented, and they were not Jewish. The next day I went back to my father to ask him. He would not answer me. How could he? He was, of course, trying to explain anti-Semitism in a way that taught us pride in our people. But I was already proud to be Jewish. I never once felt shame about being a Jew. Anti-Semitism bothered me, but it did not hurt me in a deep way.

At school, some of the teachers were anti-Semitic. There was one teacher who would assign seating based on our test grades. The child with the highest grade would get to sit in front near the teacher's desk. Then number two, number three, and so forth. One time I had the third highest score on the test. But the teacher still made me sit in the back of the classroom because I was Jewish. I complained to a classmate that I should be sitting in third seat rather than last. The girl told the teacher, who was furious and punished me by making me go to school on our off-day for a whole month. In those days, we did not have school on Thursdays. We had school on Saturdays.

Another teacher showed her anti-Semitism by refusing to call on me. When I raised my hand to answer a question, she would ignore me. One time I thought she had called on me and I started to answer. *"Assiets toi!"* she barked. ("Sit down!"). After class, the teacher called me over. "Next time you will wait until you are told to speak," she scolded. I apologized, but it made no difference. At least she did not shame me in front of the other children.

When you are a child, you are marked by experiences like that. You never forget them, even as an adult. It made me feel like an outsider. The Christian kids did not want to be friends with us. Even after the war had ended, I once started to make friends with a Christian girl who lived nearby. Each day, we would walk together to the railroad station and then return. After two weeks, the girl abruptly said, "My parents told me they don't want me to be friends with you."

I could not understand why she changed so suddenly. So I went to my mother and asked her. *Maman* looked at me with surprise, "You don't know?"

"Is it because we are Jewish?" I asked.

"Yes," she said, as if it was obvious. Experiences like that discouraged me from trying to make friends. It was better to be alone. I realized that it was pointless to try because no matter how nice you are, or polite, or bright, or cultured, it did not matter. If you were a Jew, you were always an outsider.

Fortunately, I found a best friend that never disappointed me – my piano. My parents had bought a piano when I was 8 years old. Rose, Eugenie and I all started playing at the same time. At first, my mother tried to give us piano lessons. She had attended a music conservatory in Russia. But it is very difficult for musicians to teach instruments to their own children. I know because I grew up to be a piano teacher myself.

Maman established a time for each girl to practice piano before we went out to play. Rosa went first, then Eugenie, then me. I loved to play piano. I would often go to the piano in the dining room and start to play. If I was dusting, I would see the piano and want to play. Sometimes I would just pass by the piano and stop to gaze at it. I would tell myself how lucky we were to own a piano. Mozart and Chopin, Beethoven and Mendelssohn, and especially Bach, every day. To play piano, I was in heaven.

There was only one time that I did not want to practice piano. My sisters had gone outside to play and I wanted to play too. My mother said, "No, you cannot go out to play until you finish practicing." I was defiant and started to leave. When *Maman* came after me, I started to run. She must have been drying dishes in the kitchen because she had a dish towel as she chased me around the dining room table.

As it turned out, I was the only child to stick with the piano. *Maman* also tried to start my little brother on violin, but he would not practice. The teacher said Arnold was talented, "but if he does not want to practice, you cannot force him." *Maman* and the teacher gave up on him.

When I was nine years old, we moved to another apartment above a bakery near the eastern corner of *Place Duroc*, the town square. Our address could be either 7 *Rue des Prêtes* (meaning "priest") or 7 *Rue Thiebaut II*. There were three apartments over the bakery and ours was in the middle of the three, one above and one below us. The bakery store was in the front. The bedrooms for the bakers were above the ovens in the back, behind a courtyard. It was a beautiful beautiful apartment with a long narrow hallway connecting the kitchen to the bedrooms. Best of all, we could always smell bread baking.

Such was my life in lovely Pont-a-Mousson. Family, school, piano. Who could have ever guessed how the war would change everything?

CHAPTER THREE

The German Invasion

In France in 1939, we did not know the name of Hitler, not yet, but we were well aware of the rumblings of war. Talk of war was in the newspapers, in the cafés and in our home. My parents would talk about the German threat to Europe, and how the Nazis despised the Jews – but they would discuss it in Russian or Yiddish so that we children could not understand. Though they tried not to frighten us, we could sense their mounting dread. We were not surprised when the Germans invaded Poland in September 1939 and that France and England declared war. Still, we felt safe in France, 650 miles away from the fighting.

Then, beginning on May 10, 1940, the Germans launched the war against France and England. First, they attacked through the Netherlands and Belgium in the north. The German army easily crushed them and by June 5, 1940, the blitzkreig smashed into northern France and swept quickly westward toward Paris. By June 14th, the Germans had captured Paris. This was the kind of dreadful news of defeat that we were hearing in the weeks before the Germans invaded our hometown. In our part of France, the German Army held a defensive position and did not launch its attack until June 14th. Four days later, on June 18, 1940, the German Army captured Pont-a-Mousson[1]. I was 11 years old.

The warplanes and bombing began well before we ever saw a German soldier. It was terrifying. We could hear the grinding roar of warplanes diving in, then the great thump of bombs that rattled the windows and china. One of the first targets to be destroyed was the bridge over the Moselle that connected the two sides of Pont-a-Mousson. Now the only way to get across the river was in rowboats. Later in the war, bombs destroyed one corner of *Place Duroc*, smashing many houses and arcades near the Town Hall and leaving a big deep crater.

The bombings nearly always occurred at night so we put blankets over the windows and were forbidden to use the lights. When the air-raid siren would wail, we were instructed to hurry into the basement. Early in the war, we were given gas masks because the Germans were said to drop bombs with poison gas. Later we were also given cotton and a special liquid. This was an extra precaution in the event that a gas mask would not work properly. We were told to wet the cotton with the liquid and hold it over our noses.

One night, there was an air-raid siren and our family ran into the basement along with the people who worked in the bakery. In the rush, my mother could not find her gas

---

[1] On June 18, 1940, advanced units of the German 212nd Infantry Division with a motorized artillery battery captured Pont-a-Mousson without French opposition. Elements of the French 26th Infantry Regiment surrendered to them.

mask. Then a bomb thundered somewhere nearby and a fellow from the bakery said that the Germans were dropping gas bombs on the city. My mother believed him and panicked. "I'm fainting, I'm fainting," she cried. She was holding her nose while we hunted frantically for the liquid and cotton balls, feeling blindly in the blackness. Eventually we found the cotton balls on the other side of the basement.

When we heard the rumor that the invading Germans were going to kill everyone, terror gripped the people of Pont-a-Mousson. My parents, like many citizens, decided to flee. My father knew a French soldier of Russian descent named Nicholai, who sometimes came to our home to talk Russian. Nicholai arranged for another soldier to pick up our family with a military ambulance. In the dark of night we climbed into the back of the ambulance, which was almost pitch black inside because there were no windows. Papa was supposed to follow us on his bicycle, but he could not keep up and we lost him. The ambulance driver drove us to the city of Toul, which is about nineteen miles southeast of Pont-a-Mousson, and parked in the square. There he abandoned the vehicle because Toul was being bombed. But he left us locked in the back! We could not escape. It was terrifying because we could see nothing, but we could hear and feel the tremendous explosions outside. Every time that a bomb would explode, the ambulance would shake and we would scream.

Eventually the ambulance driver returned. Since Toul was being bombed as badly as Pont-a-Mousson, we decided to go back home. He drove us back the next day.

We stayed in Pont-a-Mousson for only one more day and decided to flee again. This time nearly everyone was in a panic and were fleeing the city en masse. People took whatever precious belongings they could and fled westward to escape the invading German army. We quickly packed every suitcase we could and joined the mobs of refugees that clogged the westward road as far as we could see. Adults, children, horses, carts, bicycles, carriages – the whole city of Pont-a-Mousson. Since we lived on the west side, we did not have the added problem of getting across the river without a bridge. Papa again took his bicycle and we followed him on foot with our heavy suitcases. We had no idea where we would go. We had no friends or relatives to run to. All we could do was follow the throng and hope for the best. But we soon lost Papa in the chaos and the masses of French refugees.

We continued walking on our own – *Maman*, Rosa, Eugenie, little Arnold, and myself. Eventually, we came to a village where we approached a farm and asked for help. The woman was very kind. She fed our family along with two other families and allowed us to spend two days and two nights in her barn. We slept on the hay with the horses, thankful to have shelter and food. On the third day, the woman at the farm said, "You can all go home now because I just found out that the Germans are very kind and care about everybody."

So we started the long journey back to Pont-a-Mousson. As the refugees returned eastward, German trucks and military vehicles were rumbling westward. The people had to move out of the way or be crushed. It was also dangerous because warplanes were still bombing the roads. When the warplanes came, everyone would drop their suitcases and packages and run to the nearest ditch for protection. The bombing attacks sounded exactly like you hear in the movies. Roaring and screaming and explosions. It was absolutely terrifying, especially for children. Rosa was 15, Eugenie was 13, I was 11, and Arnold was only 6.

One time a German airplane swooped down and strafed the refugees with his machine guns. People screamed and we all ran for cover. Some were killed. It was a nightmare. I can still remember the dogs were howling. It was a strange eerie howl like I've never heard before or since. They say it is the unique howl of dogs when they smell death all around.

Thankfully we made it safely back home. (Later my father returned on his bicycle.) But Pont-a-Mousson had changed. It was now an occupied city. We saw a regiment of German soldiers marching in perfect formation, guns on their shoulders, raising and crashing their boots in unison like some monstrous machine. The looks on their faces were like masks. My mother started to cry, so we started to cry. It seemed like the Germans were crawling all over our beautiful little city – like a colony of huge gray ants.

This was a very frightening period, especially because warplanes were still bombing the city. Luckily I only saw one person killed. I was walking on the *Boulevard de Riolles*, when a warplane dropped a bomb about forty feet away. I leaped to the ground and felt the earth bounce. I saw a woman thrown by the explosion. I wanted to run to help her, but I was too frightened. I couldn't breathe. Instead I ran home as fast as I could to tell my mother about the fallen woman. She said, "You did the right thing," but I still felt guilty afterwards. I was only 11 years old and so scared, but I felt that I should have gone to help the lady. Even today, over 65 years later, I can see her fall and I feel badly that I did not run to help her.

France surrendered to the Nazis on June 25, 1940. The bombing ceased[2]. We tried to resume life as it had been before the war. Papa went back to work in the iron foundry; we returned to school; I returned to my piano. It was much the same except for the presence of the occupying army. We would see German soldiers in the cafés, or standing guard, or simply strolling around Pont-a-Mousson. Occasionally, there would be blocks of fifty or more soldiers marching together. One time my sister Rosa and I were standing outside our apartment on the corner at *Place Duroc* and *Rue Thiebaut II*. A passing German soldier winked at us. My sister looked at me and hissed, "Oh, the gall he has to do that." We hurried back home and never again stood on a street corner in Pont-a-Mousson.

We would have liked to avoid the Germans altogether except that the army requisitioned the bakery below our apartment every Thursday. The soldiers would take over the entire bakery, do their own baking and load their own trucks. We would see them in the courtyard and encountered them in the hallway. The German soldiers did not know that we were

---

[2] Given its proximity to Germany, Pont-a-Mousson was the target of periodic Allied bombing throughout the war.

Jewish so they were polite to us. In fact, the officer in charge would always give two loaves to my mother.

As the summer of 1940 passed, the Germans were puffed up with their military successes in Europe. They had easily conquered ten countries and, in August, began bombing Great Britain in preparation for crossing the English Channel. One day we were leaving our apartment and we ran into the German officer in the hall. With an arrogant smile, he declared that, "You know, soon we will march into England."

My mother looked at him calmly and replied, "I don't think your boots are high enough. You'll have wet feet."

The German officer bristled at the insult. He glared at *Maman* and did not say another word. After that, the officer stopped giving us bread and ignored my mother. But it showed the arrogance and confidence of the Germans at that time. They were sure they would conquer the world.

I wanted only to conquer my piano pieces. My piano teacher hosted a recital every year. This time I was the last student to perform and I earned a standing ovation. Papa was so proud that he rewarded me with my first trip to Paris. Papa arranged for us to stay with a friend. He knew this woman and her husband when they had lived in Pont-a-Mousson. The husband was a Jewish tailor named Pierre Leibowitz[3]. He had tried to hide from the Gestapo, but he was discovered and arrested. Later, he was deported to the death camp at Auschwitz. His wife was a Christian of German descent named "Marie." She closed the tailor shop in Pont-a-Mousson and moved to Paris to open a café. There she rid herself of her Jewish married name and took her husband's French name of "Pierre."

So my father said, "We will go and visit Madame Pierre." It was just my father and I, riding the train to Paris. I stayed with Madame Pierre and her boyfriend in the apartment over her café, while Papa stayed at a nearby hotel. Her apartment was lovely and they lived like they were wealthy. I shared the bedroom with Madame Pierre's daughter, who was about three years younger than I. There was something about Madame Pierre that I did not like from the start, but it did not spoil my pleasure. The trip was thrilling. Paris was enormous and gorgeous. I felt like a happy ant looking up at the magnificent buildings. Since it was wartime, we did not visit many tourist sites. Mostly, we played games like dominos. Still, Paris was the most exciting place I had ever seen.

Back in Pont-a-Mousson, the Germans built a wooden footbridge across the Moselle River so that the people could cross back and forth. The footbridge ran parallel to the destroyed bridge, about twelve feet over the water. You could see the rushing current between the gaps

---

[3] "Pierre Leibowitz" is a pseudonym, not his real name. A pseudonym is also used to conceal the identity of his wife, "Marie Pierre." For legal reasons, the names of all individuals appearing in this book are pseudonyms rather than actual names (except for Ida's family members).

in the floorboards and you could easily fall through the side railings, which consisted of just two thin horizontal boards. I had to cross that footbridge every day to go to school – and I was always petrified. The footbridge was only a block and a half from our home and the school entrance was located at the opposite end on the *Saint Martin* side. That flimsy footbridge seemed like it was ten miles long – with every step teetering on the edge of a deadly fall. When the other boys and girls discovered my fear, they would run close to me on the footbridge and start jumping up and down on the slats. I would scream and cling for life – but this would make them laugh and jump harder. Everyone made fun of my fright. What could I do? One time I tried to run across the bridge quickly. But I tripped on the jagged slats and fell. I grabbed the boards in terror, looking down at the surging river. After that, I would always walk slowly – but I would wait to make sure that no one was on the footbridge and that no children were close enough to run onto the bridge to scare me.

In 1941, the Germans issued ration cards for all the citizens of Pont-a-Mousson for items like meat, bread, sugar, and butter. But it was not until June 1942 that the Nazis began to pick out the Jews for persecution. That was the month that every Jewish family in Pont-a-Mousson was ordered to report to Gestapo headquarters. As Jews, we knew where the Gestapo headquarters was located and would steer clear of it. But now we had to go. The Gestapo knew exactly how many Jews lived in Pont-a-Mousson, their names, and where they lived. Every Jewish adult and child was given three yellow stars of David with "*Juif*" (Jew) written in the middle. The Nazis ordered us to sew the yellow stars onto our clothes and wear them every day – or else. Our family walked home in silence.

That evening, my father made a fateful decision. He declared that, "I will not sew Jewish stars on my clothes. If I do, they will fire me from the foundry. I have to work or we can't survive." Then he turned to my mother. "And do not sew any Jewish stars on the children's clothes either."

Even though disobedience would risk arrest and deportation, my father weighed the options and believed that we would be safer if we were not marked as Jews. My mother was the only one in our family who wore the yellow stars on her clothes. As children, we did not question Papa's dangerous decision. Our safety was reliant on our fellow citizens. We heard stories of people in Pont-a-Mousson, who threw rocks at the Jews who wore their yellow stars. It would only take one person to report us to the Gestapo – a neighbor, a coworker, a merchant, a schoolmate. Anyone could denounce us in a moment of anger or because of an anti-Semitic urge.

The other Jewish people in Pont-a-Mousson obeyed the order to wear the yellow Jewish stars. Several Jewish families had already fled to the south of France when the Germans invaded and never returned. After France surrendered in 1940, the Nazis set up a puppet government in southeastern France called the *Régime de Vichy*. Some Jews thought they would be safer in Vichy because the Nazis did not have full control there. But, in 1942, the Nazis arrested and deported any Jew anywhere in France who was not a French citizen[4]. This was the Nazis' way to track down the Jews who had already fled to France from Germany and other countries.

Beginning with the order to wear the yellow stars in June 1942, the Nazis intensified their persecution of Jews in France. Now Jews were prohibited from waiting in line to receive rations or to shop before three in the afternoon. If you were caught, you could be arrested. *Maman* would get up at five in the morning to get in line. Most Christians were kind to her and would allow her to stay in line. If a German soldier or French policeman came by, some would even hide her because she was wearing the star of David. Still, there were a few times that some townspeople would be mean and insult her: "You dirty Jew, what are you doing here? Get out of here!"

Though we did not wear our Jewish stars, we definitely changed our ways. We lived cautiously. Jews were prohibited from public entertainment, so we stopped going to the movies.

If we went outside to play, we stayed close to home and avoided the street. If we saw German soldiers – and they were everywhere during the war – we would move aside and walk slowly, staring straight ahead. We would never run or hurry because it might look suspicious. We never did anything that could draw attention to ourselves.

As early as 1941, we began hearing rumors of mass slaughters of Jews in Poland. The Nazis would first make the Jewish men dig a grave pit as long as a city block. Then they would order the Jews to stand along the edge and would shoot them into the pit. Then the next group of Jews would be forced to cover the bodies with dirt – before they, too, were massacred. We did not hear of such atrocities happening in France, but we knew there were collaborators and we had to be careful of everything we said or did. We did not dare to speak to anyone. We lived each day with a constant feeling of dread – as if we knew it was only a matter of time before disaster struck.

---

[4] Nazi Germany invaded the zone under Vichy authority in November 1942. For the next two years, until November 1944, the Vichy government tried to protect Jews with French citizenship from deportation – by sacrificing "foreign" Jews instead.

CHAPTER FOUR

The Lecher

Our worst troubles began in May 1942 when the scar-faced Gestapo man came to our apartment to arrest Papa. *Maman* said that the scar-faced man was a coward and would never return. For over a year, it looked like that might be true. Life went on as normal – though with added apprehension. I immersed myself in my piano. Nothing, not even the trauma of playing Strauss for the scar-faced man, could diminish my great love of music. I continued my piano lessons and practiced every day.

In July, my piano teacher held her yearly recital. I was voted the most popular performer. When we arrived home, my mother proudly announced that I had won the event. Papa, who could not attend for some reason, was thrilled! "You know what, Ida," he declared, "you and I are going to go to Paris again!" This would be my second trip to the magnificent city. Once again, Papa arranged for us to stay with his friend Madame Pierre and her boyfriend in their apartment above the café. On July 18, 1943, my father and I took the train to Paris. It started as an ideal vacation. We enjoyed a wonderful trip to the zoo. We walked around Paris to see the sites. At night, I slept in their apartment and my father slept in the hotel across the street.

Then, on the third day of our stay, my father received an urgent telegram from my sister telling him to return home immediately. Papa did not want to cut my vacation short, so he said, "You can stay here a little longer and I'll go home." The telegram was open on the counter in the café. I could have read it, but we were taught that you should never touch anything that is not intended for you. So I did not know why Papa had to depart so abruptly. I did not ask. But Madame Pierre saw the telegram and knew the reason: the Gestapo wanted my father.

As soon as Papa left, an old man began to fawn over me. He was a friend of Madame Pierre, probably in his 60's, who was always hanging around her café. I had met him before, but now that Papa was gone, he was constantly trying to get close to me. At first, it was three of us – Madame Pierre, the old man and I. We went to the famous cathedral of Notre Dame. Madame Pierre removed her bracelet and dipped it in the holy water to bless herself. But then she disappeared, leaving me alone with the old man. He took me to the horse-races. He took me shopping in Paris. He bought me an umbrella, a scarf, and handkerchiefs. He pressed close to me and was overly nice. He even proposed to take me to Monte Carlo, Nice and the French Riviera. He said he wanted to make me happy. But his attention made me extremely uncomfortable. At age 13, I still knew nothing of the facts of life. I had no idea why this old man was being so attentive and buying me gifts.

That evening, after we returned from shopping, Madame Pierre's daughter saw the gifts that the old man had bought for me. She started to scream in a jealous rage. She was so upset that I gave her everything that the old man had bought for me. I did not want his gifts. I did not want his attention either.

I felt more and more uneasy as the old man pressed me to go away with him. Since Madame Pierre was the only adult I could turn to, I went to her and asked for help. "Why is he buying me all these things?"

"Because he likes you very much."

"And he wants to take me to Monte Carlo?"

"Go," she advised, "you will have a better life."

"A better life?" I replied. "I want to be with my mother and my family. I don't want to go to Monte Carlo."

I knew something was seriously wrong. I did not know what this lecher intended to do to me, but I sensed serious danger. I quickly decided to get away. In the evening, I caught the next train to Pont-a-Mousson.

As an adult, I see Madame Pierre and the lecher as the height of evil. They both knew that my father was being sent to a concentration camp. They both knew he would probably never return. They conspired to take advantage of my father's imprisonment and my separation from my family. In fact, after the war, the Chief of Police told my father that it was Madame Pierre herself, who informed the Gestapo where her Jewish husband was hiding. She was responsible for his arrest and death.

As for the lecherous man, I encountered him again after the war. I was attending the music conservatory in Nancy at the time. Each day I would ride the train from Pont-a-Mousson to Nancy. One day my class was cancelled and I had to wait for the train. There was a café near the railroad station and I saw some of my classmates there. So I went over to say hello – and there he was. He recognized me and extended his hand in greeting. I refused.

I would always see him sitting at that same café by the Nancy railroad station, always fawning over the girl students. To avoid him, I avoided that café and those girls. When I told my father, he went to the café and confronted the lecher. Papa said, "You know, I can have you imprisoned for what you wanted to do to my daughter."

Eventually that awful man was caught. My father went to see his criminal trial. Papa did not want me to go to the trial so that I would not hear anything more about this man's sexual depravity. In the end, the lecher was sent to prison for selling some other young girl into prostitution. That was what he had planned for me. If I had gone to Monte Carlo with him, or if I had listened to the advice of Madame Pierre, I would have never seen my family again. I was just a child of thirteen. How could someone betray her own Jewish husband to be deported and killed by the Nazis and be ready to sacrifice the innocent child of a Jewish friend who was likely to face the same fate?

*   *   *

It was such a relief to get back home safely, but my mother looked terrible and Papa was gone. "Where's Papa?" I asked her.

"He's working," she replied, as if everything was the same. Yet her face was strained.

Later that day, I was walking through town and encountered another Jewish girl. "It's a shame about your father," she remarked.

"What is a shame?" I asked her. "What do you mean?"

"It's a shame that your father was sent to a concentration camp."

I was stunned with horror. I had no idea. I immediately ran home and dashed up the stairs to our apartment to find *Maman*. I was crying as I asked her for the truth.

"Yes, it's true," she cried. We both cried. I learned that Papa had been ordered to report to a French prison in the city of Metz, which is 18 miles north of Pont-a-Mousson. My sister Rosa accompanied Papa on the train to Metz. Papa was imprisoned on July 22, 1943 – for being a Russian Communist, not for being a Jew. About two weeks later, Papa was deported to Drancy, the largest concentration camp in France located just outside of Paris. It appears that the Nazis never figured out that my father was Jewish. He was saved by the fact that, twenty two years before, some German immigration officer had changed his Jewish name of Goffmann to the German-sounding name of Hoffmann. I later asked my father if he had denied that he was Jewish in the Drancy concentration camp[5]. I asked him a few times, but he would not answer. I am certain that Papa would have never denied his Jewishness except under those circumstances, but I suppose he thought it would hurt me to hear that he had.

At the time, of course, we knew nothing of Papa's fate. He was gone and we had to

---

[5] Located in a northeastern suburb of Paris, Drancy was the largest and most famous concentration camp in France. Originating as a public-housing project in 1932, it was used for police barracks before the war. Following a large-scale raid of French Jews throughout France in August 1941, the Nazis began to use Drancy as a concentration camp. The five-story U-shaped complex was designed to house 700 people, but typically held about 4,500 prisoners. The conditions of the camp were crowded and brutal, including the practice of immediately separating small children from their parents. Most victims did not stay for long at Drancy, however, because its primary function was to serve as a temporary transit camp from which Jews from all over France would be deported to Auschwitz for extermination. Initially, the camp was operated by French police under Nazi direction. From July 3, 1943 until liberation on August 17, 1944, the German SS took over direct operations at Drancy as part of the Nazis' accelerated program of mass executions. Of the 70,000 Jews who passed through Drancy, 65,000 were sent to death camps, including 11,204 children. The vast majority died during the last year of operation under the Nazis, when more than 61,000 Jews were deported from Drancy to Auschwitz-Birkenau. Ida's father was imprisoned at Drancy for over a year and was among the 2,000 survivors to be liberated in 1944. He probably survived because he was classified as a political prisoner (Communist) rather than a Jew. Ironically, over 60 years later, the Drancy building is still used for its original purpose of public housing.

find a way to make ends meet. As a Jew wearing a yellow star, *Maman* could never find a job. So my oldest sister Rosa quit school to take an office job at the iron foundry where my father had worked. We were able to get along on Rosa's salary and family savings. Still, we needed to be careful with every penny. We could no longer buy clothes, but we could eat adequately. Like other French citizens, we had ration cards for meat, bread, sugar, and, on rare occasions, butter. We would get one box of sugar each month, which *Maman* would use to barter with the baker's maid to get bread. Bread was our main food.

There was one occasion when a farmer friend of my father gave us a fifty-pound bag of kernel corn as a gift. In Europe at that time, no one ate corn. Corn was used only to feed farm animals, so we had never cooked or eaten corn before. We disliked the odd taste of the corn, but we were glad to receive the food. We ate the entire bag. Once my sister tried to make a cake from grounded-up kernels. It was awful, but we moaned, "Oooo, oooo" as if it were delicious.

The worst consequence of having less money was that I would be forced to stop my beloved piano lessons. By this time, I was the only child still taking piano lessons. We did not know how long the war would go on and it was a luxury that we could no longer afford. So, with a grieving heart, I trudged to my last piano lesson and faced my piano teacher. "Mademoiselle Fariel," I lamented, "I'm sorry, but I have to stop my piano lessons."

"Oh no, Ida, why?"

"Because my father was arrested and taken to a concentration camp. And my mother cannot afford to pay for my lessons anymore."

Mademoiselle Fariel looked at me with kindness. She was a devout Catholic. "I will see you at the end of the week just like we always do. You will continue your lessons and I will not charge you any money. You are so talented that God would punish me if I did not give you piano lessons." So, thanks to the generosity of Mademoiselle Fariel, I was able to continue my piano lessons free of charge. She even risked arrest by giving me lessons since Jews were forbidden by law to take piano lessons. So, once a week, very early in the morning, I would walk to my secret piano lesson with Mademoiselle Fariel. At 6 am, it was usually still dark and I was afraid to walk on the streets alone. But I was determined to repay her kindness by making the most of my lessons. It was a luxurious treat to take piano lessons during the war. I practiced for hours every day – and I loved it.

Other people also showed kindness and helped us to survive. Our neighbors knew that we were Jews and did not report us to the Gestapo. Our landlords, who were two sisters, risked trouble for renting to Jews and allowed us stay in our apartment. The owners of the bakery downstairs, Madame Bolair and her husband, later helped us to escape from the Nazis.

But our most surprising help came from a German soldier, who worked in the bakery downstairs. Every Thursday, when the German army requisitioned the bakery, he would conceal fresh loaves of bread under his coat and sneak into the courtyard to hide them. Then he would whistle a tune as a signal to my mother to come down to get the bread. My mother would sit near the window at the hour when the Germans would load the fresh bread and prepare to leave. The soldier knew we were Jewish and he risked a lot to give us bread. He could not do it every week, but he did many times between the summer of 1942 and spring of 1944. I wish I knew his name. We truly appreciated his generosity.

There was another German soldier who was kind to us. He was a very tall, very handsome German officer. He would often come to visit the French woman who lived in the apartment above us. Although her own husband was a prisoner of war, she had fallen in love with the enemy. The handsome officer would often pat me on the head when I was playing outside. He knew that we were Jewish and he protected our secret. Eventually, the French woman bore the German officer's child and, when the German army retreated from France, she followed him to Germany with their child.

As for Papa, we knew nothing of his fate for a long time. There was no way to try to contact him and no way for him to write to us. During that time, we continued to hear rumors of mass murder of the Jews of Europe. We knew of the perils of concentration camps and worried that Papa might die or be killed. Papa did succeed in getting one letter to us during the time that he was imprisoned at the concentration camp at Drancy. It was dated March 5, 1944, a Sunday. The letter itself is quite odd. Since Papa could not write well in French, he must have dictated it to someone else, which could explain some of its unnatural expressions and strange content. Or the letter may have been written as a coded message or warning. It is a mystery. Though we had not and could not send letters to Papa, he refers to letters and packages that he had received from us. The most peculiar feature was that Papa refers to underwear three times, saying once to send it and once to <u>not</u> send it. This was the letter:

Hoffmann No. 115   *Paris*   *March 5, 1944*

My dearest,

I have received your letters, and the two packages. But once more, I beg you not to send me anything, only for what I would ask you. Tomorrow I will advise you about my package of underwear.

In your next package, I would like you to send me my sweaters, my underwear and my woolen socks, also my blue shirts. Nothing else. Please send them to me.

In the meanwhile, if you can find them, send me tobacco and cigars.

About the package of underwear, don't send it unless I ask you for it.

I was very happy to receive a letter from Rosa. She could write more often, once a week at least. I also received two letters from Eugénie and one from Ida, also from Arnold. I hope he is now a true big boy, and he will do everything that is possible to be very good. Also work hard in school. I wish him a good birthday and all my best wishes.

I am always in good health, everything goes as well as possible. I don't need anything, they are very nice to me. But despite all this, I wait impatiently to be able to hug you all very tight in my arms. Monsieur Linger has not written to me, as of yet. I have not received his letter.

Say hello to our friends, and to you all my best kisses.

Hoffmann

As it turned out, we did not receive this letter from Papa – because it arrived shortly after we had fled from our home to escape the Gestapo. Madame Bolair, the baker downstairs, saved the letter to give it to us after the war. The "Monsieur Linger" mentioned in the letter was a teacher at our school.

CHAPTER FIVE

Escape From the Gestapo

We lived quietly in the apartment over the bakery at 7 *Rue des Pretes* until March 1, 1944. I remember the date because it was my brother Arnold's tenth birthday.

I was in school. It was a Wednesday. I was suddenly called out of class and sent to the Dean's office. I was afraid that I was in trouble. But the Dean spoke to me in a soft, kind voice. "I want you to go home immediately and warn your mother," he said. "Tomorrow the remainder of the Jewish people are going to be deported to a concentration camp." I was stunned and scared. By "the remainder," the Dean meant any Jews who had not been deported and were still living in Pont-a-Mousson. The Dean had gone out of his way to save me and my family. I later learned that Monsieur Linger, the teacher named in Papa's letter, had warned my middle sister Eugenie as well.

I hurried straight home, crossing the scary wooden footbridge to the *Saint Laurent* side of Pont-a-Mousson. As I was walking, I noticed Monsieur Louire driving his van. He owned a bakery in town. When I looked through the window of his van, I could see three large lumpy sacks of flour. I don't know how, but I instantly knew that there were girls hidden inside each sack. I had the strongest intuition that it was a Jewish girl in my class and her two sisters. Later, I learned I was right. Monsieur Louire had concealed them inside the flour sacks and was driving them to a safe house.

When I told my mother about the deportation, her face turned pale and all she could say was, "Oyyy…" Our family had just one evening to decide what to do. Should we flee? Should we stay? Should we hide? *Maman* was overwhelmed by the situation. She said, "I don't know who to ask. I don't know who to trust. We have very little money left. I don't know what we should do…"

After struggling with the decision, *Maman* resolved that we should stay, but she would try to find a refuge for Arnold. So she took him to the home of two Christian friends of my father. Monsieur and Madame Herlin were wealthy from their businesses in scrap metal and petroleum. They lived in a grand house in Pont-a-Mousson. You would enter through a gate and walk another half block to reach the house.

"Can you keep my boy for a few days?" *Maman* asked.

The Herlins did not hesitate to say yes. In fact, they sheltered Arnold until the end of the war. The Herlins were well-respected and wealthy, but they could have lost everything for the sake of my little brother. They treated Arnold wonderfully. For safety, Arnold rarely left the house except to go to school – but he was able to continue going to school like a normal boy. Since he was confined to the house, Arnold spent many hours in the kitchen with Madame Herlin, watching her cook. She was a chef and he was fascinated by the chemistry of cooking. In fact, this experience led him to become a professional chef as a adult.

Thankfully, given the status of the Herlins in Pont-a-Mousson, no one reported my brother to the Nazis. But there was one incident that could have been disastrous. Arnold punched another boy at school for calling him a "dirty Jew." Arnold slugged him so hard that he gave the boy a black eye. The boy's mother came to the Herlin's house to complain. She threatened to report them to the Gestapo for hiding a Jew. She said, "You know what I can do." Mrs. Herlin stayed calm. She knew this woman was a heavy drinker so she quietly slipped two bottles of fine wine in the woman's pocket and her bag. The angry mother walked away happy.

*   *   *

After finding a safe place for Arnold, my mother returned home. She decided that we would wait in our apartment. She said, in Yiddish, *"Madloch, wussen zehn feh zehn."* "Girls, what will be, will be..." My sisters and I were awake all night, worrying about what would happen to us tomorrow. We talked in whispers about being deported to a concentration camp. We wondered where we would be sent and if our family would be separated. No one slept. We did not pack suitcases or prepare in any way. We just watched the clock as we sat and talked through the long hours of darkness – *Maman*, Rosa, Eugenie and I.

We knew the Germans always came to arrest Jews at five o'clock in the morning. And sure enough, as the hour came, we heard footsteps and a knock at the door. We stood up, broke into tears, and said goodbye to each other because we expected to be separated. Then *Maman* opened the door. But it was not the Nazis! It was Madame Bolair, the blond assertive woman who owned the bakery downstairs. She spoke in a frantic voice, "Hurry, hurry, the Germans are coming to get you! I'm going to hide you."

In that split moment of time, we abandoned our plan to surrender. We quickly ran out and followed her to the ovens where they baked the bread. Madame Bolair hid my mother and two sisters in a small wooden pantry. But there was no room for me. Instead, she gave me a white apron and said, "Quick, go down to the basement. If they come down to the basement, act like you are working. You can put potatoes in a basket, or move coal, just do something." I scrambled down the stairs and quickly tied on the apron. Then I waited there with my heart pounding in my throat.

Meanwhile the German soldiers marched upstairs to our apartment. When they saw that no one was there, they came down to the bakery and asked Madame Bolair if she knew where we were. In her fright, she said, "They went to the school to say goodbye to the Dean

33

of the school." She shouldn't have said that because the Germans went straight to the Dean to find us. When he said he did not know where we were, the Gestapo threw the Dean in prison for two weeks. In truth, he wasn't lying. He had no idea where we were.

I knew nothing of this as I waited nervously in the basement. But the Germans never came downstairs. They placed one soldier to guard the front of our apartment and left. We remained hidden in the bakery all day long. My mother and sisters stayed in the pantry and I pretended to work in the basement. Later, my mother and sisters moved from the closet to the baker's bedroom and hid there. Throughout the long day, Madame Bolair or her husband would come and tell us what was happening with the Germans.

My family and the bakers talked about what we should do. We had not planned to escape so we had run out with nothing but the clothes on our backs. We had no food, no money, no identification cards, nothing. Most of all, we needed our coats because it was still winter.

That evening, my little brother Arnold suddenly appeared. He had returned by himself to find out what happened to us. This made it even more urgent to get away. Later in the evening, the Germans changed the soldiers guarding our apartment, which gave Madame Bolair an idea. There was a young French woman living on our street, who was known to be friendly with the Germans. Madame Bolair lied to the young woman, saying that the German guard was interested in meeting her. The woman walked up to the soldier in a flirtatious way and said, "Come here, Hans." This was not his real name, of course, but the soldier readily followed her. Madame Bolair's plan worked perfectly. The young lady had no idea that she was being used to lure the German guard away from our apartment. This gave my little brother Arnold just enough time to sneak into our apartment to grab our winter coats. There was no time to get anything else.

Now, with our coats in hand, we devised a plan. It would be too conspicuous to travel together so we decided to split up. I suggested that my mother and my sister Eugenie go to the farm of a school friend. I had once spent a week of vacation there and her parents had treated me well. It was agreed that Arnold would return to the Herlin's house by himself. Then my mother and Eugenie would go to my friend's farm. As it turned out, my friend's family was too afraid to hide them, but they were able to find shelter at another farm.

Meanwhile, my oldest sister Rosa and I went to her friend's house to hide. We stayed there for the night and the following day. Our plan was to escape to Paris and seek help from Madame Pierre. Though I disliked her and dreaded the idea of seeing the old lecher again, we could think of no better option. So Rosa and I made it to the station in Pont-a-Mousson and took the evening train to Paris. We rode all night, thankful that no one asked for our identification.

In the morning, Rosa and I walked to Madame Pierre's café. Rosa explained that we had escaped deportation and were hiding from the Gestapo. "Can you help us?" Rosa asked.

"No," replied Madame Pierre.

Rosa explained that we were desperate and had very little money.

Finally, Madame Pierre relented. "I'll put you up for one night in a hotel that I know. You can come back for breakfast tomorrow morning, but then you will have to go somewhere else."

The "hotel" was a run-down building on a tiny side street that was used as a brothel. We went to our room and locked the door. We were relieved to have a safe place to rest since we had not slept for two nights. But then, around midnight, we were awakened by a loud knock at the door. We looked at each other, but did not answer. Someone knocked again. We still did not answer. Then a man's voice barked, "I'm a policeman, and you better open the door. I know you girls are in there."

Rosa and I held hands as we fearfully walked to the door and opened it. It really was a policeman. He studied us closely and asked, "What are you doing here?"

"We are Madame Pierre's nieces," we answered. I'm sure we looked scared and innocent. Rosa was nineteen and I was fifteen.

"Ohhh," he said, "then you better lock your door. And don't open it for anyone else."

Even today, I do not understand why the policeman came to our door. But after that, we were too frightened to sleep. This would be our third night in a row without sleep.

In the morning, we went to the café and ate breakfast with Madame Pierre. Rosa told her that our father had been taken to Drancy concentration camp one year before. "We don't know if he is still there or not," Rosa said.

"Well, why don't you go to Drancy and see if he is still there?" suggested Madame Pierre.

We nodded. We did not suspect that Madame Pierre was misleading us with bad advice. We took the train to Drancy concentration camp, which was in the suburbs of Paris. It was Friday, March 3, 1944. We walked into the little office at the main gate. We could see the guards and prisoners inside the barbed wire fence. The German guard asked what we wanted.

My sister Rosa replied, "Is there a Monsieur Hoffmann in the camp?"

The guard looked through a dossier and found our father's name. "Yes," he said, "he is here. Who are you?"

"His daughters," we replied, excited that Papa was still alive and we would get to see him.

The German soldier went to the phone, cranked the lever, and instructed someone to send my father to the office. A short time later, I was looking through the office window and saw Papa walking toward us. He was wearing wooden clogs and a plain prison uniform without stripes. He was so skinny that he looked like a different person. In my excitement, I ran out of the office and into the camp to greet my father. I was so happy to see Papa that I was unaware of the guards who were pointing their machine guns at me and yelling, "Halt! Halt!"

When my father saw me, he started to cry. "So they caught you, too?" he lamented.

"Not really," I replied. "Let's go to the office to talk." I did not want to make a scene in front of the guards.

So we walked into the office. Then Papa saw Rosa. He was delighted to see her too, but then greatly alarmed. "What is happening, Rosa?"

Rosa tried to quickly explain our situation and why we were in Paris. We spoke very softly in French. Fortunately the German guard was not listening. "We don't know where to go."

"I'm going to give you the name and address of a lady in Paris, who is not Jewish. Her husband and son are in the camp with me." Papa must have developed a close friendship with them because he immediately knew the name and address. "But you must leave right away."

Papa knew it was urgent to get us out of the concentration camp. He pulled two onions from his pocket and gave one onion to each of us in case we were hungry. Given his condition, he certainly needed the food for himself, but he insisted on giving the onions to us. He repeated his warning, "You must leave right away. If the guard realizes who you are, he will arrest you." Thankfully, the German soldier was still not paying attention and had left the prison gate unlocked. Rosa and I departed right away, holding our breath until we had walked safely out of sight of the guards.

As we rode the train from Drancy to Paris, we realized how very lucky we had been to see father and not be captured. We walked directly to the address he had given us. She was a sweet and very distinguished lady of wealth named Madame Charon. She treated us wonderfully from the moment we arrived, feeding us and feeding us again to relieve our hunger. We enjoyed staying in her magnificent apartment, filling ourselves with food. But Madame Charon warned us that we could only stay a few days "because the Gestapo sometimes comes to check up on me." Her husband and son were also imprisoned at Drancy and she was under suspicion. We stayed for three glorious days, although my sister insists that it was a week.

During our stay, Madame Charon arranged an office job for Rosa in a small convent on the other side of Paris. At age 15, I was still too young to get a job. Then Madame Charon recommended the name of another woman who would be willing to hide us.

Off we went. The next woman was also very nice and welcomed us to stay with her. Everything seemed fine until night. That is when Rosa and I began to hear her talking out loud. We knew that she lived alone and no one had come to the apartment, so she must be talking to herself.

We looked at each other. "Do you think she's cuckoo?" Rosa asked.

"I don't know," I replied, although I shared the same idea.

"We'll stay the night and leave in the morning," Rosa decided.

The next day Rosa asked the woman if she could recommend someone else who could help us. She seemed perfectly normal in the daytime. She gave us a new name and address and we departed once again. We later found out that this woman was a spy in the French Rèsistance – and we had been hearing her communicating with England using a secret radio.

Our next benefactor was a prostitute, who lived in a filthy apartment filled with so much junk that we could barely squeeze inside the front door. Clothes were scattered over the floor. Everything was in disorder and dirty. We told her about our predicament and poverty. "Don't worry," she said, "you could make a lot of money in my profession. You should do what I do." I had no idea what kind of work she did, but judging from her messy apartment, it could not be good. Later, when we were alone, I asked Rosa what profession the woman was talking about.

"Don't think about it," Rosa replied. Since I knew nothing of the facts of life, Rosa did not try to explain what a prostitute is. "We'll go somewhere else in the morning."

The next day we left. I decided to return home to Pont-a-Mousson. I missed my mother and I did not want to be a burden to my sister. Rosa was not making enough money to support both of us. So I said, "I am going back to Pont-a-Mousson to try to find *Maman*." I knew it was dangerous to return to my hometown where so many people knew I was Jewish, but I could think of nowhere else to go. I was only a child.   What else could I do?

So I took the night train for home. There were seating compartments within each train car. Although the car was crowded, I found a seat in one of the compartments. More people continued to board, including an elderly woman who was forced to stand in the aisle. I offered my seat to the old woman and went in search of another for myself. The next train car looked inviting so I went inside. It was much nicer and there were plenty of seats in the compartments. I did not understand that the crowded car was for French citizens, while this car was reserved for Germans and their French employees. I simply wanted to find a seat and this car was deserted. So I said to myself, "I'm going in."

There was one man inside the compartment. He wore the clothes of a factory worker and looked pleasant. "*Bonjour, Monsieur,*" I said.

"*Bonjour, ma petite,*" he replied. ("Hello, my little one.").

I sat by the window and covered the side of my face. I did not want him to recognize that I was Jewish. The train pulled away and we rode in silence.

About an hour later, a French policeman and a German soldier entered the compartment to check our tickets and identification cards. My stomach dropped to the floor. Even if I had my identification card, it would have been stamped "*Juive*" (Jew). I was caught. I knew I would be arrested.

The policeman went to the stranger first. He pulled out his identification card and showed it to the policeman. The officer nodded, then asked for mine.
I could not move, frozen with fright. But before I could think of anything to say, the stranger spoke up. "She is my niece."

"Oh," the policeman said, and the two officers walked out. I could not believe my fortune. I had not even spoken to this stranger, yet he had just risked his life for me.

After the officers left, the stranger turned to me. "Are you a Jewish girl?"

"Oh no, Monsieur," I said without hesitation.

"You can tell me. I just helped you."

I shook my head again. I did not dare to trust him. I thought he might report me or even shoot me.

He persisted. "You can tell me!"

"Sorry," I replied, "I am telling you. I'm not Jewish..."

After that, we never spoke another word for the rest of the ride. I had been incredibly fortunate. This kind stranger had risked his life to save mine – the life of a total stranger, the life of a Jew.

*　　　*　　　*

I arrived in Pont-a-Mousson at five o'clock in the morning. Although I was back in my hometown, I had nowhere to go. I had no home, no family and no friends that I could turn to. I did not know where my mother and sister were hiding. I only knew that my brother Arnold was under the protection of the Herlins – and I did not dare to go there for fear of being followed.

To avoid being seen, I decided to take the *Boulevard de Riolles* instead of *Rue Victor Hugo*, the main street of Pont-a-Mousson. This was a mistake because I encountered dozens of workers on their way to the iron foundry. Though I kept my face lowered, one worker saw me and made an expression of surprise. Obviously, he thought that my family and I had been arrested and deported along with the all of the other Jews of Pont-a-Mousson. He was probably pleased to see me, but I was terrified to be recognized and immediately started to run.

I ran down the first side street I could find, desperately seeking a place to hide. Thinking quickly, I realized that the closest possible place of refuge was a friend of my sister Eugenie. I rang the doorbell. When her mother answered the door, she was alarmed to see me. "Hurry, hurry," she whispered, "run away as fast as you can. My husband is a collaborator."[6]

So I again started to run. I ran blindly, with no idea of where to hide. I saw the neighborhood grocery store on *Place Duroc* where we used to shop. It was still too early to

---

[6] A few years ago, I learned that my middle sister and my mother had also sought refuge at this house and had stayed there for a day or two. They escaped when they learned that the husband was planning to report them to the Gestapo. His wife deterred him by saying, "If you do that, I will go to the French police after the war and tell them what you did." This gave them time to flee.

be open, but I rang the bell and waited, panting. Monsieur Poincare came to the door. He knew my family was Jewish and recognized me right away. "Can I hide here for the day?" I asked in a desperate, breathless voice. "Just for the day. Then I will leave tonight." Where, I did not know.

Monsieur Poincare said, "Yes," and took me upstairs to their apartment. I sat in the kitchen all day long, miserable with hunger, while the Poincares worked downstairs in their grocery store. They had not thought of offering me food and I was taught to never take anything without permission. So I just sat there in the kitchen, stomach growling, and tried to devise a plan. I thought about my life before the Nazis and my life now. I thought about the last day of school when the Dean sent me home to warn my mother. Then I remembered hurrying home and seeing Monsieur Louire that day, driving his bakery van with the three lumpy sacks of flour. If he had been hiding Jews inside those sacks as I had guessed, then maybe he would help me too. His bakery was a short distance from the grocery. I asked Monsieur Poincare if he would contact Monsieur Louire.

Later that afternoon, Monsieur Louire arrived with his bakery van. He came upstairs to the apartment with an empty flour sack, put the sack over me, hoisted me over his shoulder, and carried me out to his van. I breathed through a little air hole that he had made for me. I had no idea where he was taking me and I did not ask. He drove for about three quarters of an hour, but it seemed like an eternity for me inside the flour sack.

Finally the van stopped and Monsieur Louire turned off the engine. He helped me out of the flour sack. It was like landing in paradise. I found myself at an enormous farm belonging to a farmer named Monsieur Touval. I saw about twenty people approaching to see who had arrived – and one of them was my mother! When *Maman* saw me, she ran to me. What a glorious moment. We hugged. We kissed. I was so happy. Monsieur Louire knew right where my mother was hiding because he was in the French Rèsistance. Soon I found that my sister Eugenie was hiding there too! It was a true family reunion.

I stayed at the Touval farm for the next three weeks, sharing a little room with my mother and enjoying the plentiful food. I learned that many of the farm workers were really fugitives or members of the French Rèsistance, who were merely pretending to do farm work. We were the only Jews hidden on the farm. At night, Allied airplanes would often fly over, secretly dropping parachutes loaded with supplies for the Rèsistance. One night, my sister and I were the first to run to one of the mysterious parachutes. We never actually saw what the planes were dropping, but it must have been weapons, ammunition, radios and such. This was happening in the middle of March 1944, a few months before the Allies would land at Normandy. After the war, a dressmaker made us blouses from one of the parachutes. They were surprisingly comfortable and quite warm because they were not porous.

For a brief time, life was again simple and safe. I appreciated the joy of freedom and the blessing of my family more than I ever had before. I was flooded with good emotions – the joy of a child restored to her mother's arms; the relief from constant fear; the reassurance of a small, safe place. With so many feelings pouring out of me, I felt the need to express them. For the first time in my life, I was inspired to write poetry. My first poem recalled the frightening solitude of the train ride from Paris to Pont-a-Mousson, hiding my Jewish face, and fearing recognition as I ran from house to house, seeking refuge:

HIDING MY FACE	MON VISAGE, J'ESSAYAIS DE CACHER
I waited at the station for the train	*A la gare, le traim j'attendais*
I was forced to travel alone	*Seule, j'etais obligée de voyager*
Sitting near the window	*Assise prés de la fenêtre*
I had to appear calm	*Calme, je devais paraître*
I tried to hide my face	*Mon visage, j'essayais de cacher*
I arrived in Pont-a-Mousson	*A Pont a Mousson, je suis arrivée*
Not knowing where to go	*Sans savoir chez qui aller*
I had to protect myself from the Gestapo	*De la Gestapo je devais me protéger*
Afraid to be recognized, I trembled	*Peur d'être reconnue, je tremblais*
I ran from house to house	*D'une maison a l'autre je courais*
I was hidden by Monsieur Poincare	*Par Monsieur P. j'ai été hebergée*
With his family, I spent the day	*Avec sa famille, j'ai passé la journée*

I wrote three more poems during the three wonderful weeks that I spent on the Touval farm with *Maman* and Eugenie. In one poem, I wondered, "Is it my nature" to have "such a sad face." In another I imagined "happy mortals without wings," who are "forced to stay here on earth."

My fourth poem was written on the day before I left the Touval farm. It is unlike my other poems that survived the war because it was the most fanciful. It played with romantic themes like any normal teenage girl might do – if she were growing up in a normal world. In my poem, I dared to let myself be a girl again and fantasize about doing "foolish things for the sorrows of love." For a brief time, I could believe again in a good life.

But it was a mistake to let myself feel safe.

CHAPTER SIX

The Lion Lady

The next morning, a car drove into the Touval farm. As usual, the workers gathered from around the farm to see who had come to visit. A middle-aged couple seemed to have come to buy a chicken, or butter, or some other produce from the farm. My mother and I stood among the others, quietly observing as the couple prepared to leave.

Then the farmer's wife suddenly faced me and said, "You are going with them."

My heart stopped. It could not be true. Go with these strangers and lose my mother again?! I was stunned. No one had said anything about leaving to my mother and I. All we could do was look at each other. We did not speak. We did not hug. We did not cry. We just looked at each other in anguish. *Maman* gave me a little money and I dutifully climbed into the back seat of the car with the two strangers. Then we drove away.

I remained silent during the car ride. Neither the woman nor the man spoke to me. They made no attempt to be friendly. There was no conversation, not even an introduction of names. I did not know who they were, or where we were going, or why I was going with them. I was in such despair that I could think of nothing except losing my mother. I had nothing. I had no change of clothes. These would be the only clothes that I would wear every day for next nine and a half months.

We drove for a long time and the couple continued to ignore me as if I did not exist. I studied the woman and her cold eyes. She was striking in appearance, even frightening. Though she was middle-aged, she had jet black hair, which was styled to stand very high in the front and sides. I had never seen such hair. I said to myself, "If her hair was gray, she would look just like a lion." From then on, I thought of her as *Madame Delion*, "the Lion Lady." Her attention-grabbing hair style reflected her personality. She was haughty and self-righteous, selfish and cruel. She always acted like a big shot.

Eventually we reached their home, a large beautiful apartment in the town of Laxou, which is just a few miles west of the city of Nancy. They obviously had enough money to live in luxury. They certainly could have afforded a maid. But this, I soon learned, was what Madame Delion intended for me. I would be their slave. I would work without pay and without meals. I would be confined to the apartment at all times unless I was given permission to run an errand. And if I dared to complain, Madame Delion made it clear that she would report me to the Gestapo as a Jew. My young life was under her total control.

Madame Delion and her husband had two sons and a little girl. I never knew the name of the oldest boy because they never seemed to use it. The second boy was always called by his nickname of "*Prince*." Likewise, the little girl was always called by her nickname, "*Princesse*." So I never learned the actual name of any of the children. It did not matter because the children ignored me just like the parents did.

Madame Delion showed me a small room in the attic where I would sleep. It had crude walls, a squared ceiling, and a single window. The furnishings consisted only of a broken metal bed and a chair. The bed had no mattress, just a thin cover over metal springs. It was more comfortable to sleep on the floor on a blanket. It was the only blanket I had and there was no heat in the attic. Some boxes and bags were also stored in the other half of the attic, but I never looked at them. I would always go straight into my little room.

Madame Delion immediately expected me to do housework. "You have to clean," was one of the few sentences that anyone said to me that first day. I had never been taught to clean because my mother did the cleaning in our home. Madame Delion put me to work in the kitchen where I tried my best to clean the gas stove. I did not know that I could remove the metal grill to clean inside the burners. Madame Delion erupted in a rage and slapped me! The blow staggered me, but I was too astonished to feel the pain. It was the first time in my life that I had ever been struck in the face. I just stood there in horrified disbelief as the sting and blush rose on my cheek. But I did not cry. To this day, I am very proud of myself for not crying. Beginning that first day, Madame Delion slapped me in the face every single day. She beat me day after day, and often twice or three times a day – but I defiantly refused to cry. I would stand and receive her blows, but I refused to give her the satisfaction of knowing that she could hurt me.

At first, I thought I could avoid her violence by learning to do the housework correctly. But it was soon clear that nothing would please Madame Delion. It did not matter how hard I worked or how thoroughly I cleaned, she would slap me in the face, both sides. The only good thing that I can say about her was that I never saw her strike her own children.

I also had to learn to live with hunger. I was given no food. One night, as I was cleaning the dishes, I scraped a tiny piece of food from the bottom of a pot and ate it. Madame Delion went into a rage. "Don't you ever do that again!" she shrieked. Nothing, not even a speck of a discarded meal, was allowed for me. She did not care that I must have been starving to do something so desperate. Instead, she became obsessed with preventing me from salvaging any scrap of food from their meals, especially the food frequently left over by her little daughter. Madame Delion did not trust me to do their cooking and she watched my every move to be certain that I did not pilfer food or retrieve some scrap from the garbage to eat. (I would starve before I would ever steal food or eat from the garbage). I quickly realized that I was expected to somehow provide my own food. Fortunately, I had the tiny bit of money that *Maman* had given me.

During my first week, Madame Delion sent me to buy Clorox bleach, which was very difficult to obtain during the war. I had to walk a very long distance, tramping for two hours to reach the store to buy eight one-liter bottles of Clorox. Now I faced a terrible problem: How was I going to carry the heavy glass bottles all the way back? With four bottles in each arm, I started. The bottles of bleach were so heavy that I could only walk for twenty feet before I would have to stop to rest my aching hands and shoulders. Given this excruciating pace, I could not imagine how I would ever get back to Laxou.

Then, as I was resting by the roadside, a gray car drove past. I could see it was a German car with several German soldiers. The car suddenly stopped and parked on the side. My heart pounded in fright as a German officer got out of the car and began walking toward me! Then I recognized him. It was the very tall, very handsome German officer, who fell in love with the French lady in the apartment above us in Pont-a-Mousson. Even though he had treated me kindly in the past, I was still afraid that he was going to arrest me now.

"What are you doing here?" he asked.

"I'm on vacation," I lied.

The German officer looked down at me for a long time, then asked, "Where is your mother?"

"I don't know."

Again, he looked at me for a long time. He knew I was Jewish, of course. Then, in German, he said, "*Pass auf.*" ("Watch out."). He walked back to the car and they drove away.

I grabbed the heavy bottles and started again. Stopping and starting, a thousand times over, I somehow managed to get back to the apartment – and collapsed.

After a week of misery with the Lion Lady, I turned to the only friend that I could – my poetry. This poem was the first of many that I wrote during my long ordeal with Madame Delion. It shows my overwhelming sense of desolation at that time.

MY SOUL CRIES

My soul cries

I am really afraid

The world is without flowers

The sun without light

The heart of the world is made of stone

The night will end

Tomorrow will start

MON ÂME PLEURE

Mon âme pleure

J'ai vraiment peur

Le monde est sans fleurs

Le soleil sans lumière

Le coeur du monde est fait de pierre

La nuit finira

Demain arrivera

With this poem, I discovered a medicine to help soothe my pain and loneliness. I was an orphan living under constant surveillance and danger of attack. Poetry became my secret way to retain my dignity and sense of myself. But this, too, required stealth and cunning because I was not allowed to have a pencil or paper. One day Madame Delion caught me taking paper from the waste basket and so she tried to tear up my poems. From that day forward, I had to keep my poetry hidden.

I could not hide my poems in the attic because Madame Delion often searched my room. I don't know what she hoped to find. I had no possessions and no food, not even a drawer or suitcase to put things in, if I had. I suppose her purpose was to catch me with stolen food or something to punish me for. She had given me a key to lock the door, but she would use her own key to enter. I used saliva to put a blade of grass over the door so that I would know when she had been prowling. But Madame Delion soon discovered my trick and beat me severely for my cleverness.

In the beginning, I would hide my poems in my socks and underwear. But after writing a dozen poems, I needed another way to store them. I began to pin the poems inside my clothes using pins that I could pilfer when I darned socks for the family. But my solution was far from perfect. The pins would often prick me if I sat or moved in a particular way – and then I would have to bite my tongue to conceal any expression of pain.

I also learned to be alert to the times that the children did their homework because they would often discard paper when they made mistakes. This became the source of my precious paper. But I still needed a pencil. One day, I dared to ask the middle child, Prince, if he could spare a pencil. Reluctantly, he gave one to me. Thankfully, he did not tell his mother.

The following poem reveals another trick I found to cope with my misery – music. I longed for my piano like I longed for my family. I was incomplete without music. So I began to pretend that my chair in the attic was my piano at home. I would hear the music in my head as my fingers danced on the invisible keys: Mozart and Mendelssohn, Bach and Beethoven, Chopin's waltzes and *My Yiddishe Mama* were mine again, my small escape from the grim silence of my confinement.

IN THE ATTIC

I climbed to the attic
As usual without food
No one to speak to
Alone with my thoughts
The chair takes the form
Of my piano
For the moment,
I don't think of the Gestapo
I make believe I am playing
Chopin's waltzes
The music helps me
To forget my hunger
Tomorrow, the sun will show itself
In the attic, the window will open

AU GRENIER

Au grenier je suis montée
Comme d'habitude sans manger
Personne avec qui parler
Seule avec mes pensées
La chaise prend la forme
De mon piano
Pour le moment
Je ne pense pas a la Gestapo
Je fais semblant de jouer
Les valses de Chopin
La musique m'aide
A oublier ma faim
Demain le soleil se montrera
Au grenier la fenêtre s'ouvrira

I was only allowed to leave the apartment to shop for their groceries and to take Prince to his tutor. Madame Delion sent me to the grocery during my first week. It was less than two blocks away. I was so thrilled to be released from confinement that I was caught off guard by the grocer. As soon as I walked into the store, the grocer stared at me. "Oh my God," I said to myself, "he knows I'm Jewish."

I summoned my courage to approach the grocer and handed him the shopping list. "I know your mother," he said.

"I'm sorry," I replied, "but I am an orphan."

"No. I know your mother," he said again. "You have two sisters and a brother, and your father is in a concentration camp."

He clearly knew my family, but I was too scared to acknowledge it. So I repeated myself. "I'm sorry, I am an orphan."

The grocer persisted. "I know the farm where your mother and sister are. Would you like the telephone number?"

I shook my head and repeated myself once more. "No, I am an orphan."

Realizing that I would not confess, he wrote the telephone number on a piece of wrapping paper. I pretended to look at the number as if I was not interested, but I memorized the number.

As soon as I returned to my attic room, I wrote down the telephone number. I did not say a word about this to Madame Delion. Every day from that day forward, I wanted to call that number, especially when I was feeling most alone and desperate. I would debate with myself. "Should I call? Shouldn't I call?" But I feared that it was a Nazi trap. So I did not call.

Another day I was walking to the grocery and a woman stopped me on the street. "Why is your face is so red?"

I was surprised by her question. Then I realized that she must have recognized the red marks on my face from being beaten by Madame Delion. I quickly tried to think of something to say. "I eat a lot of fruits," I blurted out. I don't know how such an idea came into my mind.

The woman walked on and I took a deep breath of relief. The red marks on my face had remained long enough to be seen hours later. It shows how hard Madame Delion would strike me. Though her blows were hard enough to knock me down, I would not protect my face. I would stand and receive each blow – and never ever shed a tear. I had no choice but to endure her cruelty. It was the Lion Lady or death by the Nazis. The best I could do was to anticipate the attack and brace myself for the crack of her hand against my cheeks. There was no escaping her abuse because she would use any reason to beat me. One time I believed that I had done a perfect job of cleaning. But she found a thin edge of dust hidden under the edge of the countertop – and promptly delivered her nasty reward.

There were only two days when Madame Delion did not beat me. Two days out of more than a hundred days. The first time was the day that I was mending their socks and clothes. She liked the way I mended the socks. She said, "It's a work of art." Mending socks was the one domestic task that I been taught in school.

As the weeks passed on, starvation stole the flesh from my bones. Not once did the family offer me food or money to buy food. Madame Delion made sure that I would get nothing, not even scraps from their leftovers. Although I had been strictly raised to never steal, in this extreme case, I believe I would have yielded to hunger and taken a bit of food – if I could have. There was no opportunity. Madame Delion locked all the food in cabinets and guarded the garbage can. If I had ever found a plate of unguarded crackers or cookies on the table, I still would not have eaten one because I would be sure that Madame Delion had counted them and it was a trap.

There was one time that my hunger pangs overcame my pride. It was one of the rare occasions that I was left alone in the apartment. I knew that Madame Delion locked the crackers in a particular top drawer. Ashamed that I was forced to steal food, I said to myself, "I'll only take one cracker. She won't miss just one cracker." I tried to think of a way to open the locked drawer. I removed the drawer above and tried to reach under, around and up. But the cabinet was solid wood.

So how did I eat? On the day that Madame Delion took me from the farm, my mother had quickly divided the little bit of money that we had. I had nothing but the clothes I wore, my winter coat, and this small sum. I had no choice but to stretch my money for as long as I could – and there was no way to know how long that might be. When I was sent to the grocery, I could only buy fruit and vegetables because other food required a ration card. I would try to buy enough vegetables to last three days, which would cost about 55 *centimes*. I subsisted almost entirely on rutabagas, carrots and potatoes, which I would sneak back to the attic. Since I had no running water, I would put saliva on my finger to scrub the dirt off and then I would eat the vegetables raw. It is difficult and unpleasant to bite into raw potatoes and rutabagas, especially rutabagas, which are very hard.

A handful of vegetables each week did little to calm my hunger pangs. Given my situation, I was constantly hungry and thinking about when I might eat again.

PERHAPS TODAY I WILL EAT

Last night I dreamed
I got up, tired, disoriented,
I looked around me
The end of my voyage seems so far away
I would like to escape
Not to stay here and languish
I try to think
I don't even know what about
Perhaps today I will eat
I know it won't be the case
I have to force myself to survive
I would like to have books
I see the birds from my window
They are masters of their own destiny
I envy their liberty
One day, I hope to have mine
Whatever happens, I have my pride

PEUT ÊTRE AU JOURD'HUI, JE MANGERAI

La nuit dernière j'ai rêvé
Fatiguée, desorientée, je me suis levé
J'ai regardé autour de moi
La fin de ma randonnée me parait si loin
Je voudrais pouvoir m'enfuir
Ne pas rester ici a languir
J'essaye de penser
A quoi je ne sais même pas
Peut être au jourd'hui, je mangerai
Je sais que ce ne sera pas le cas
Je dois me forcer a survivre
J'aimerais avòir des livres
Je vois les oiseaux de ma fenétre
De leur destin, ils sont maîtres
J'envi leur liberté
Un jour, j'éspère avòir la mienne
Quoi qu'il arrive, j'ai ma fierté.

"My pride." It is remarkable that pride – my refusal to cry when Madame Delion beat me; my refusal to steal or beg for food to the point of starvation – could be a source of so much strength and determination. Hunger is a dreadful thing. It is like having a vulture's claws digging into your shoulders and never letting go. The vulture is always in the corner of your eye, weighing down on you. All you can do is numb yourself – by shutting down all feelings and trying not to think about your hunger pangs. But, like pretending to play piano, it never truly works; it only distracts you from the suffering. I was miserable every day, losing weight week by week, turning into skin and bones.

After enduring two months with the Lion Lady, I was desperate to see *Maman*. But I knew it was impossible. In the same way that writing poetry helped me to escape my misery, writing this letter helped me to imagine my mother's face and hear her singing Tosca to me.

Chère Maman,

This afternoon I feel like writing a letter to you. I know I won't be able to send it because I don't know where you are. I have been living with a family for the last two months. Father, mother, two boys and a little girl. I don't know how much longer I can stay. I work all day as a maid. Do you remember when you were cleaning, I wanted to help you. You would say to me, "You will have time to work. Housework is for mothers." I also darn their socks and mend their clothes. The lady says she likes the way I darn the socks. Other than giving me orders, the family never speaks to me. Only when she needs something or tells me what to do. She does not give me any food and I have to wash the dishes. I am always hungry. I am starting to accept my destiny. I am only 15 years old. I am alone, very much alone. I see your face. I hear you sing Tosca. I remember when I was playing piano. You would stand behind me. You never tired of listening to me play. You would always say to me, "Very good." You were so proud of me. For the holidays you would take us to the dressmaker for new clothes. You also bought us new coats. We would take walks on the Boulevard. I could continue but it makes me so sad. Do you know who I think about? My sisters and my brother.

Chère Maman, forget what we had before. I am afraid we will never see each other again. The country is so big. Oh, the other day I saw Jean Gorin. He was visiting the people next door. He was looking at me, but I hid my face. I did not want him to recognize me.

Chère Maman, if I am able to find a piece of paper, I will write again....

I folded my sad letter, knowing I had no address to send it. I pinned it inside my clothes with my secret poems. More than sixty years later, it bothers me that my letter did not mention my father. I knew that Papa was in the concentration camp at Drancy. Perhaps, in my own overwhelming despair, I had given up hope that he was alive. My unsent letter also mentions Jean Gorin. He was a nice boy from my elementary school in Pont-a-Mousson, who I had not seen in many years. If I did not have to hide, I would have loved to greet him.

Such was my existence under the Lion Lady – unceasing hunger, daily beatings, thankless labor, and the ache of loneliness. My naiveté blinded me to another one of Madame Delion's selfish pleasures. One afternoon I was in my attic room when I was startled by an urgent cry from downstairs. Madame Delion ordered me to come down immediately. I quickly scrambled down the stairs and she promptly pushed me into the bathroom. "Whatever you do," she hissed, "don't let Monsieur Delion in the bathroom! Lock the door and stay in there until I say so – and don't let him in the bathroom for <u>any</u> reason!"

I locked the door as ordered, confused and anxious, wondering what was happening. Suddenly a nearly naked man popped out from the shower curtain! I jumped back and nearly screamed aloud, but he motioned for me to keep quiet. "Sssh! Ssssh!" My heart was pounding from fright. Standing there in his undershorts, I recognized him as a man who had visited the apartment before – usually after Monsieur Delion had gone to work. Today, after finishing lunch at home, the husband had returned unexpectedly to retrieve his briefcase – and had nearly caught Madame Delion in bed with her secret lover. I knew absolutely nothing of the facts of life, but I understood enough to know she was doing something very wrong. The incident was never mentioned again and I knew to keep silent.

I also kept silent about another sexual incident. In addition to my occasional trips to the grocery, I was allowed to leave the apartment once a week to take Prince, the middle son, to his tutor. Prince was not a little child. He was only a year younger than I, but I was responsible for walking him to his lessons and bringing him home. It was a fifteen minute walk and he had a one hour lesson. Never once, on any of those walks, did Prince speak a single word to me. I suppose that Madame Delion ordered him to never speak to me – just like I had been ordered to never speak to anyone in the family.

I certainly never spoke of what happened the first time that I took Prince to his tutor. I walked into the room and the tutor greeted me. He was a chubby older man with a goatee and round grinning face, who looked just like Burl Ives, the actor and singer. Within a minute of meeting me, and with Prince standing right there in the room, the tutor groped my breast! I jumped back and ran from the room. I never again dared to enter the tutor's room. I would walk Prince to his lesson, walk back to the apartment, and return to get him at the end of the hour. But I never went inside the tutor's room again.

And so the lonely, miserable days dragged by. I continued to write poetry to sustain hope, including this excerpt from one of my poems called "A Day Will Come."

I think, I think, I think	*Je pence, je pense, je pense*
The nightmare that pursues me	*Au cauchemar qui me poursuit*
I am afraid, I cry, I am hungry	*J'ai peur, je pleure, j'ai faim*
Until now, I still have strength	*Jusqu'a maintenant, le courage, je l'ai encore*
I am alone, always alone…	*Je suis seule, toujour seule*

CHAPTER SEVEN

Alone in the Wilderness

After three long months with the Lion Lady, my little bit of money was nearly gone. I had tried to stretch each penny for as long as I could, but now my situation was desperate. I was already as thin as a skeleton and weighed just sixty-six pounds. I might have enough money for another week of raw vegetables and then I would be facing total starvation.

Then, one day in late June 1944, Madame Delion abruptly announced that they were going on a family vacation. Of course, she did not trust me to stay in their apartment while they were away, so they drove me to an isolated farm and dropped me there. I had no idea where I was. In that region of France, there are many farms hidden among the forests, isolated from other farms and villages. I was supposed to stay there for two weeks until they returned from vacation. After just three days, however, the farmers suddenly cast me out. They said that other people were asking who I was. Although they never said so, I believe they were afraid to be caught harboring a Jew.

I left the farm with no idea where to go. I was only fifteen and utterly lost in the wilderness of Meurthe/Moselle. All I could do was wander the deserted roads through the thick forests. Eventually I devised a plan. I would look for farms and if people were working outside in the fields, I would approach them and ask for work.

After trudging for several miles, I found a farm and knocked on the front door. It was opened by an older couple. "I am an orphan," I said, "and I am looking for work."

The wife was friendly and both were polite, but the husband had a mean face that made me nervous from the start. The woman asked me, "How good of a cleaner are you?"

"Very good," I replied.

"Then we can give you work."

I enjoyed a full meal and then began cleaning. That night, I slept in the stable with the farm animals. The cows were on one side and the horses were on the other side. The stable was not unpleasant, but the animals were constantly making noises. I had never spent time with farm animals before and I could not sleep because the animals would make deep belly sounds like "mmmmh, mmmmh." Since I could not sleep, I started counting the number of animal sounds. By daylight, I had counted nineteen! I remember because it is the same number as my birthday.

The next day, I worked again and they fed me well. It felt good to have food in my belly and to be free from the Lion Lady's bite. After the evening meal, I was washing the dishes while the farmer and his wife were talking in the kitchen. "Ohh, if I could just find myself a Jew," the husband said, "we could get a new tractor."

Painting by Ida Hoffmann Firestone of the farm
where she slept in the stable with the horses and cows.

Fear shot up my spine. "Oh my God," I thought to myself, "if he discovers that I am Jewish, I'm going to be his tractor!" At that time, the Germans offered a bounty to French citizens if they reported a place where Jews were hiding. My knees were shaking as I finished washing the dishes. I knew I must flee. I went to the stable and waited for nightfall. The stable door was very close to their bedroom window and I could see the candlelight when they went to bed. As soon as the light went out, I sneaked out of the stable.

I hurried down the dirt road in the darkness, trying to get as far away from the farm as I could. I stumbled again and again, unable to see in the blackness. The tall thick trees of the surrounding forest spread over the country road like witches' fingers and blotted out any moonlight that could light my way. This was my first time in a forest at night and I was absolutely terrified. After I had run as far as I could, I decided to hide in the woods. I attempted to enter the thick black mass of trees, but I quickly lost my courage. The darkness seemed total inside the woods. Every black form was a threatening monster. I retreated back to the road.

There I stayed, clinging to a tree by the edge of the road, praying for the light of morning. I remained by that tree through the entire next day as well. I was utterly alone. Not a single person or vehicle came by. To pass the time, I watched the clouds or counted blades of grass. Then I shivered through another endless, frightening night in the forest. That was all I could bear. The forest was scarier than the Gestapo. At the first light of dawn, I set off again to wander the roads.

In this region of France, there are great expanses of forests. It can be many miles between isolated farms. This is my painting of myself when I was lost in the wilderness. The forest scene may appear tranquil and beautiful with its rich colors of late summer and fall, but

Painting by Ida Hoffmann Firestone of the time
that she wandered lost in the forest in June and July 1944.

to me, a child, the wilderness seemed infinite and hostile. Imagine that you are a child, starving and alone, with no idea of where you are, where you should go, or what will happen to you. It is utterly terrifying. Every mile feels like a thousand miles when you are lost and terrified.

I wandered for miles until I finally reached another farm. I felt such relief to find a house that I would have knocked on any door. I was surprised when a giant woman opened the door. Staring up at her enormous height and powerful shoulders, I felt tiny. "I am an orphan and I'm looking for work," I said meekly.

"Are you lost?" she asked.

"Oh no," I said, "I'm just going from farm to farm, trying to find work."

She smiled at me. "Come in," she invited, "would you like something to eat?" Right from the start, she was so good to me, like a giant angel. She gave me a lovely bedroom with a luxurious feather bed. After months of sleeping on the floor, I was in heaven. And when she found out that I love pudding, she made me pudding every day. She would do anything to make me comfortable.

The giant lady was the only stranger that I trusted to reveal that I was a Jew in hiding. When she heard the truth, she picked me up and hugged me tight. She was very strong from working in the fields each day and she nearly crushed me in her arms. "I will watch over you to the end of my days," she declared.

I believed her completely. For the first time in months, I dared to feel safe. "Oh, thank goodness," I said to myself, "I know she will protect me."

For the next four days, I lived in glorious luxury, eating my puddings, sleeping in my feather bed, conversing with the giant lady. She lived with her adult son, who was in his late 20's, but he never spoke. Maybe he talked when I was not in the room, but I never heard him say a sound. He may have been a deaf mute.

On the fourth night, I was tossing and turning in bed. I sensed something that made me uneasy. Then I happened to look at the mirror, which was mounted on the armoire. There, reflected in the mirror, I saw the son was hiding under my bed! I started to scream. The giant lady ran into the bedroom to save me. She saw her son and used her great strength to drag him out from under the bed. She was enraged, punching him as she dragged him out. She hit him over and over, but he never made a sound. A few minutes later, the giant lady returned. She stayed with me for the rest of the night to protect me.

But the morning brought bad news. "I'm sorry," she said regretfully, "but you cannot stay. I cannot keep watch on my son every hour of the day." The giant woman would have fought like a tiger to protect me from the Nazis, but she could not protect me from her own son. So I had to leave.

I said a sad farewell to the giant woman and set out once again into the vast unknown. All that day, I walked and walked, through forests and open fields. The world seemed so immense and overwhelming. As I wrote in a poem at the time, "I feel so small, I want to cry."

Painting by Ida Hoffmann Firestone of the farm
of the giant lady, who treated her with great kindness.

Eventually I came upon another farm with a couple and repeated my usual story: "I am an orphan and I'm looking for work."

The wife said, "Yes. we need somebody." So I stayed with them and worked for the next three days. Then Sunday came and the couple invited me to church with them. They did not own a car, so we walked to church together, the wife, the husband and me. In church, I tried to imitate whatever they did. If they knelt, I knelt. If they read the Bible, I made believe I was reading the Bible. But when it was time to make the sign of the cross, I did something obviously wrong. The farmer's wife suddenly glared at me. "We'll talk when we get back to the farm," she hissed.

We walked back to their farm in silence. I wondered, "What did I do wrong? What will they do to me?" I grew more nervous with each step. When we arrived at the farm, the wife took a chair and said, "You sit here and wait for us to come down." I sat. But as soon as they went upstairs to change their Sunday clothes for their everyday clothes, I slipped out of the house.

This time I was grateful for the thick dark forests of Meurthe/Moselle. I ran straight into the woods, more afraid of being caught by the farmer than I was afraid of the forest. I stayed hidden in the woods for two days and two nights, listening for the sound of the farmer or the Gestapo coming to capture me. I was so petrified that I did not think of my hunger. I found a place by a brook and thought of my dear mother:

I SEE MY MOTHER'S FACE	JE VOIS LE VISAGE DE MA MÉRE

Sitting by the brook — *Assise prés du ruîsseau*
I see my reflection in the water — *Mon reflet je voís*
I am thinking of my family — *A ma famille je pense*
Also of my childhood — *Aussi a mon enfance*
The water is so calm and clear — *L'eau est si calme et claire*
I see my mother's face — *Je vois le visage de ma mére*
Her smile and her eyes so green — *Son sourire, et ses yeux si vert*
I hear the murmur in the water — *J'entend l'eau murmurer*
The wind whispering — *Les hurlements du vent*
I must return to reality — *Revenir a la realité je dois*
I am so close to the forest — *Si prés je suis de la forêt*
I will hide among the trees — *Parmi les arbres je me cacherai*
Where I will stay the night — *La nuit je devrai y passer*
I am so afraid of the darkness — *Des ténèbres j'ai peur*
I will stay awake — *Eveillée je resterai*
I feel so sad to be alone — *Si triste, je me sens d'être seule*
Not to cry — *Pour ne pas pleurer*
I begin to hum — *Je commence a fredonner*

As the long hours crawled by in the forest, I pondered what to do. I realized that the two week vacation was over for Madame Delion. "Should I go back to those awful people? Can I bear again to be beaten every day without mercy? Or shall I go from farm to farm and risk capture by the Nazis?" So far, I had been thrown out by the first farm and had to flee from three more. Even the most promising protection of the giant lady had turned ugly. As much as I dreaded more hunger and beatings by Madame Delion, it was the only place that offered reasonable safety. I decided to go back to the Lion Lady.

I had barely enough coins to buy a bus ticket to Laxou. The bus was crowded with country folk, merrily slicing bread and munching sausages from great baskets of food. I stood because there were no seats, my stomach growling from two days in the forest without food. I watched them with envy, thinking, "How lucky they are to have such food." It smelled so wonderful.

One woman must have noticed my ravenous expression. "*Fille*, would you like some?"

My mouth watered for a slice of fresh bread. But I declined her offer. "*Oh no, merci Madame*," was all that I said. I did not dare to reveal that I was hungry. If they saw how hungry I was, they might suspect that I was a Jew on the run. I turned my back and stared out of the bus windows for the rest of the ride.

After the bus arrived in Laxou, I walked directly to the Delion's apartment. I rang the doorbell and the Lion Lady came to the door. I looked up at her familiar mane of tall black hair. "You're glad to be back, aren't you?" she snarled with satisfaction.

"*Oui, Madame*," I lied. I expected her to slap my face right there on the doorstep.

"Come on then," she snapped, "there's a lot of work to be done." She knew I must have been wandering and could find nowhere else to hide.

CHAPTER EIGHT

Caught by the Gestapo

I resumed my slave work and Madame Delion resumed beating me. I was numb with despair and growing weaker from starvation, too weak to feel the full sting of her slaps on my face. By this time, I was down to my very last pennies for food. My emaciated body moved by instinct; my mind felt thick and pressured. I was losing all hope as I wrote these lines of poetry:

So young, so alone	*Si jeune, si seule*
The hours and the days are so long	*Les heures et les journées sont si longues*
The future seems so far away	*Le future me semble si loin*
I am starting to believe in it less and less	*Je commence a y croire de moins en moins*
Tomorrow will be another day	*Demain sera une autre journée*
Is it the moment to pray?	*Est ce le moment de commencer a prier?*

About two weeks after my return, I was walking to the store in Nancy to do the shopping. I always walked with my head down because Laxou is a suburb of Nancy and people from Pont-a-Mousson often came to the big city to shop. Perhaps in my starving state, my head was hanging lower than usual that day, but I noticed a pair of shoes. "Isn't that funny?" I said to myself, "those look like my sister Rosa's shoes." I dared to turn around and look at the person wearing them.

It <u>was</u> my sister Rosa! My appearance was so wretched that she had not recognized me. I called to her, "Rosa! Rosa!" Oh, we were so happy to see each other! Rosa had returned from Paris a few weeks before because she wanted to be closer to home when liberation came. It was July 1944 and the Allies were driving the Germans eastward across France. Rosa was now working in Nancy and staying at a *pension*, which is a rooming house for girls who are visiting from out of town or attending college. I withheld the truth of my starvation and beatings. I did not want to burden Rosa with my misery. I did not even ask her for money.

When I returned to the apartment, I told Madame Delion of my fortune and asked if Rosa could come to visit me. "Never!" she sneered and ordered me to stay away from my sister.

I should have at least asked Rosa for a little money because, two weeks later, my last penny had run out. "What will I do?" I said to myself. "I have to eat, even if it is just a bit every other day. I have to eat. What will I do...?"

A day came when the Delion family went away for the afternoon. I was desperate. I decided to call the telephone number that the grocer had given me almost four months before. I dialed the number and a woman's voice answered.

"Excuse me, Madame, do you have a lady by the name of Mary living there?" I asked. "Mary" was the false identity that my mother used to hide from the Gestapo.

"Yes," she replied, "who are you?"

I did not dare to say I was her daughter. I hesitated. "A friend," I said.

"Just a moment..."

I waited a short time and who comes to the phone? *Maman*!

I was thrilled to hear her voice. And when she heard my voice, she began to scream with excitement. "Ida, where are you?! Where are you?!" she cried.

It was not safe to tell her on the telephone. But the sound of her crying caused me to break down. "I am hungry, I am so hungry, *Maman*!" I cried in return.

"Tell me where you are! I'll send you bread. Tell me where you are."

"I will tell you, I will," I replied, knowing that it was too dangerous to say it over the telephone.

Then she started to talk to me in Yiddish. She was blessing me, over and over again. She reassured me that we would soon be home together again.

"I will call you back," I said joyously in French.

We both hung up. I was ready to pop with happiness and relief. I had found my mother!

Three seconds later, the telephone rang. I lifted the receiver.

"Mademoiselle Ida, this is the Gestapo."

My heart fell to the ground. I couldn't breathe. I couldn't speak.

"You must come to the Gestapo now," a man's voice ordered. "Don't try to escape. If you do not come, we now know where your mother is."

I listened in a cold sweat as the Gestapo told me the street in Nancy where I was supposed to go.

"Alright" was all that I could say. I did not think to question if the Gestapo really knew where my mother was hiding. I figured that they must know if they had tapped the telephone. It was a trap and we were both caught.

I sat in doomed silence, waiting for the Delion family to return from their outing. About two hours later, they walked in. I faced the Lion Lady and told her what had happened. She hit me very hard. "*Sale juive!*" she screamed in my face. "Dirty Jew!" She struck me again and again. She hit me so hard, so hard. I was staggered by her blows, but I did not fall. I did not protect my face. I stood there, being beaten as she cursed at me. "Dirty Jew! Filthy Jew!" I thought she would never stop beating me.

Finally Madame Delion stopped. "Get out of here," she roared. She was afraid that now, she too, was in trouble with the Gestapo for harboring a Jew.

I left the apartment and began trudging to the Gestapo office in Nancy. It was like walking to my own execution. Each step was a step closer to death. When I was halfway there, I thought of my sister Rosa. "I have to go to my sister first," I said to myself. "I have to tell Rosa what has happened to me."

Knowing that I would see my sister made it a little easier to walk. I found Rosa in her room at the *pension*. We talked about the situation. "Don't go," she concluded. "The Gestapo doesn't know that I am here. They won't know that you are here with me. They won't find you."

"Yes," I agreed. I was still worried that the Gestapo could trace *Maman*, but I felt some ease. At least, I was with my big sister. I was no longer alone. Rosa gave me some food for my swollen stomach and I stayed the night in her room.

At seven o'clock the next morning, we were suddenly awakened by someone knocking on the door. It was the manager of the *pension*. "Mademoiselle Ida, you are wanted on the telephone."

I knew it was the Gestapo before I took the telephone receiver. The Gestapo must have called Madame Delion and she must have told them that I had a sister at the *pension* in Nancy. I faced Rosa and said, "I am going to the Gestapo."

"Then I am going with you."

"Absolutely not," I argued, "why should they catch both of us?"

Rosa insisted. "I am going."

Together we walked slowly to the street in Nancy where the Gestapo was located. But we did not know which house to go to. The Germans had requisitioned an entire street of single homes. Different signs indicated different agencies, like the "Commander," the "Feurer Commander," and the "SS." We knew that the SS were the very worst. We definitely would not go there first. We considered the choices. One house was distinguished by its window-boxes with beautiful red flowers. It looked the most inviting. So I said to my sister, "Let's go to this one."

We went inside and the German guard asked what we wanted. I said, "I was asked to come to the Gestapo."

"Wait," he said, "You'll go to room #17." It did not seem possible that there could be so many rooms in one ordinary house. Rosa and I climbed the stairs and entered Room #17. The room was about fifteen by eighteen feet wide. There was a very long table with about ten soldiers and officers and some young ladies who were secretaries. We stood close to the door, scared and silent, holding hands. My sister was nineteen and I was fifteen.

The commanding officer saw us. From his seat, he said, "Mesdemoiselles, come closer."

We took a few steps closer and froze.

He eyed us both and declared, "Aha! You are Jewish, aren't you?"

"Oh, no, sir," we said immediately.

"What are you doing here in Nancy?" he asked.

Rosa said, "I am working here and my sister is going to school."

"Where do you come from?"

"Boulogne," I blurted out. I remembered a former classmate who moved to Pont-a-Mousson from Boulogne. She had missed her hometown so much that she had described every detail to me. I had not planned to use this alibi, it just popped out. I had enough memory of the details that I could sound convincing.

The commanding officer examined us with a skeptical squint. "You can tell me you are Jewish. Nothing will happen to you."

Of course, we knew differently. "Oh, no, sir," we repeated.

Then one of the secretaries suddenly spoke up. "I know the older one."

When there are many people in a room, you can sometimes miss a face. We looked at the young woman and recognized her from Pont-a-Mousson.

"She's my best friend," the secretary continued, "We are very good friends."

The officer was very surprised. "Oh, so you are very good friends?"

"Yes," she said, "the best of friends."

The officer turned back to us. "Alright, you can go."

We left the room and hurried down the stairs, eager to get away. When we reached the street outside, the secretary ran to catch up to us. "If anyone ever tells you to come to the Gestapo," she warned us, "don't you EVER do it!" We nodded and hurried away. After the war, we learned that she had been working for the Germans as a double agent for the French Rèsistance.

We had been saved by the miracle of window boxes and a hometown acquaintance. But now where would we go? Even though the Gestapo had called the *pension*, Rosa was not afraid to go back there. She decided to return there and keep working at her job. Rosa could not keep a guest in her room and she was not earning enough money for the two of us. We thought about where I could go for shelter.

"I am going to call the telephone number again and see if I can go there," I decided.

Rosa agreed. We hugged goodbye and I walked to the train station. But when I went to use the public telephone, I realized that I had forgotten to ask for money from Rosa. I did not have a single penny.

I sat anxiously, wondering what to do. I did not dare to go to my sister in case someone was trailing me. Then I remembered a café in Nancy that was owned by some Russians. When my father visited Nancy, he would always go there to speak Russian. The Russian owners had a daughter named "Suzanne" whose husband was a known collaborator with the Germans. Nevertheless, I decided it was my only choice. "If he turns me in to the Nazis, what can I do?" I said to myself. "I am at the end, really. I'm exhausted. I'm dying from starvation. I have no money. The Gestapo is hunting me..."

So I walked to the Russian café and Suzanne was sitting there. She gasped at the sight of me. "Oh my God, a ghost!" she exclaimed.

"Suzanne," I said, "I've just come from the Gestapo. I denied that I was Jewish and they let me go. I have to make a telephone call. But I don't have any money. Could you lend me some money and I will repay you after the war."

Suzanne had become very anti-Semitic by this time and she gave me a look of disgust. "Here," she sneered, reluctantly tossing some pocket change on the ground. My pride did not matter. I gladly dropped to my knees to scrape up the coins.

Quickly leaving the Russian café, I walked back to the Nancy train station. I dialed the same number and the same woman's voice answered. I again asked for "Mary" and the woman recognized my voice.

"I have a very bad cold," I said. "Can I come and recuperate." This pretense was another spur of the moment idea. I had not planned to say it.

"Of course," she replied.

I exhaled in relief. "How can I come to you?"

"Go to the brewery in Champigneulle," she explained. "Tell them you are a relative, and they will bring you here to me."

I started immediately. It was a very long walk to the brewery, over two hours. I approached a man in the office at the brewery. He wore a beret. "I am Madame Goulin's niece," I said, "can you take me there?"

"Of course, but we are not leaving for two days. Come back in two days and we will take you there."

Two days?! I was crestfallen. Where will I go for two days? What will I do for two days? The Gestapo is chasing me. I have only ten cents remaining from the telephone call.

As I trudged back to Nancy, I came up with a plan. I would look for apartment buildings, go inside, and check for unlocked apartments. If the front door was open, I would go inside and sit on the floor beside the door. If I heard people coming up the stairs or approaching the apartment, I would quickly get up and sneak out.

I walked all night in Nancy, looking for apartments with unlocked doors. I did this for two days and two nights, finding a few places of safety. But I did not sleep nor try to sleep. I was too afraid to sleep. And I did not eat. I felt it would be wrong to take food from the strangers' apartments. Instead I would suck my thumb to create saliva in order to have something to swallow. The hours were so long, so long...

CHAPTER NINE

Liberation

On Monday morning, after two hungry, sleepless days and nights in Nancy, I walked two hours back to the brewery in Champigneulle. The man in the beret put me in his truck and we started driving. I had no idea where we were going. Our route took us through Pont-a-Mousson. I was alarmed when the beer man parked his truck outside the theater on *Place Duroc*, the big triangular-shaped main square. I was afraid to be recognized in my hometown, so I kept my head down and hid my face.

"Do you see the movie theater? Would you bring this reel of film there?" he asked me.

"I'm sorry, my ankle hurts," I lied, "do you mind if I go to the next stop?"

"Not at all," he replied and delivered the film himself.

We traveled west to an isolated farm near the little town of Limey, which is about eight miles west of Pont-a-Mousson. Like the Touval farm where I first stayed with my mother, it was a large farm and many workers approached from all directions to see who had come to visit.

Sitting in the truck, I felt a sudden urge to look at the farm house. And there in the window, I saw my mother! She was looking back at me. I jumped out of the truck and ran to *Maman*. I fell into her arms and she hugged me tight. *Maman* caressed my face, thanking God to have found me again. We were reunited at last – on August 7, 1944.

The farm belonged to Monsieur and Madame Goulin. It felt so good to be a child again, safe with my mother, but I could not allow myself to feel relief. I did not know if they would keep me here or not. I remembered the Touval farm and how my heart was broken when they sent me away with the Lion Lady. I remembered the other occasions when I thought I had found refuge – only to be forced to flee for my life.

I did not dare to get my hopes up for the approaching liberation either. The American and British armies were driving the Germans back across France, getting ever closer to Meurthe/Moselle. In the next few weeks the signs of battle increased. Fierce warplanes would suddenly roar overhead and we could hear the frequent distant thunder of cannon fire. But, in the murk of my starved brain, I could not believe in freedom. Who knew what new disaster might fall and destroy us?

By this time, I was in critical condition. I was a walking skeleton, weighing just 65 pounds. My dark curly hair hung straight down from lack of nutrition. My skin was pale and my face was gaunt with sunken eyes. Even if I was offered food, and there was now plenty at the farm, I could not eat it. My stomach had shrunken and my throat refused to swallow. My body did not trust food – like my mind did not trust freedom.

I was given a few light tasks to do on the farm, but the Goulins did not want me to do any serious work. I was obviously too weak to do much. I mostly accompanied my mother as she performed her daily chores.

Monsieur Goulin was a striking sight. He was immense, nearly seven feet tall and muscular – but kind and gentle. He always wore a little fedora on his head, which appeared comical to me given the enormity of his frame below. Madame Goulin was equally kind, but of normal size.

About two weeks after I came to the Goulin farm, I developed a terrible throbbing toothache. The pain increased as my jaw swelled. Each day the swelling was worse. Monsieur Goulin could see the problem getting worse. "You can't go on like that," he said, "the infection will spread and you could die." Something had to be done soon. Monsieur Goulin inspected my aching molar. "Well, you know you can't go to a dentist. You might be recognized. But I think I can help you. Come with me."

I followed Monsieur Goulin to the barn. As he towered over me, I wondered what the gentle giant was planning to do. He spat into his hands, rubbed them together, and picked up a pair of dirty pliers that are used to pull nails from horseshoes. I stood there, squeezing my hands together as I braced myself for the operation. Monsieur Goulin opened my mouth, grabbed the infected molar with the dirty pliers, and ripped it from my mouth. The pain was so excruciating that I nearly fainted. Blood flowed from the hole, filling my mouth.

But that was not the end. "You might have the same trouble with the molar on the other side," Monsieur Goulin concluded, "so I better pull that one out too."

Sure enough, the giant man again used the filthy pliers to grab onto my good tooth and ripped it from my mouth. It was the greatest pain I have ever experienced. To this day, I am petrified of dentists. The sight of hands coming at my mouth terrifies me. When *Maman* saw me after the operation, all she could say was, "Oy, oy, oy," over and over again.

*   *   *

During the war, the mayor of the village of Limey would come to the Goulin farm and warn the people to hide in the woods before the Germans came to search for Jewish fugitives or Rèsistance fighters. This happened shortly after I arrived. The people scattered into the forest to escape from the Germans. My mother and I did the same. As we were hiding, we were startled by the sudden appearance of a man in civilian clothes. My mother and I backed away in fear. He urged us not to be afraid and explained that he was a Russian soldier who had escaped from a German prisoner of war camp. When he realized that my mother spoke Russian fluently, they conversed. The man said that he came from a Russian border town near Germany.

Maman and I went back to the farm and informed Monsieur Goulin of the Russian soldier who was hiding in the woods. Some other workers went to find the Russian. They brought him back to the farm and gave him a room.

A few days later, the Russian soldier said to me, "I want to show you something." I followed him alone to his room, where he carefully removed his suitcase from under the bed, lay it on the mattress, and opened the lid. There on top was a German uniform! He was not Russian soldier, he was a German soldier! I screamed out loud and ran from the room. I ran to my mother and Monsieur Goulin and told them what happened. He was a German deserter, who had been posing as a Russian soldier so that he would not be killed. He used his disguise to convince French farmers to give him food. A few hours later, the imposter disappeared from the farm.

This episode, along with the approaching and increasing cannon fire, added to my anticipation of some disaster that would steal our precious freedom. It was a terrifying week. We could hear more gunfire and cannons, louder and closer now, and warplanes often roared over the farm house. We were scared 24 hours a day, but we stayed put.

One day, Monsieur Goulin received a warning telephone call. The retreating German army was burning every farm in the area to keep supplies from the advancing Americans – and they were coming toward us. Monsieur Goulin gathered all the people on the farm, including my mother and I, and had us move bales of hay in front of the farm buildings. Then he set the bales on fire so that the Germans would believe that his farm had already been torched.

But it was too late. *Maman* and I were standing in the courtyard when two massive German tanks suddenly appeared! We could have fainted from terror as the German tanks crossed the field and rumbled into the courtyard of the Goulin farm. Trying to appear calm, my mother walked to the house and entered the kitchen. I followed her. She sat by the window and began removing peas from pods, keeping her head down to hide her Jewish face. I sat too.

My mother said, "Save yourself, Ida, run!"

"No, I'm staying with you."

Meanwhile the Germans prepared to burn the farm. Outside the window, we could see two pairs of German soldiers climbing down from each tank, while two more soldiers remained on top of each turret. They were frightening to behold. Each German soldier carried a machine gun in his right hand and a grenade in his left. Madame Goulin welcomed the soldiers, offering them food in hopes of gaining their sympathy and saving the farm.

Now *Maman* began to cry. "Please Ida," she pleaded with me, "save yourself! Run!"

I could not bear to make my mother cry. I quickly took a basket and carried it outside. I walked past the German tanks as calmly as I could and headed for the barn. From there, I thought I could escape into the forest without being seen.

Madame Goulin led the German soldiers to a room on the second floor where they smoked meat and sausages. She guessed correctly that the Germans would be hungry. Madame Goulin stuffed their pockets with food and more food. They were so happy to have such excellent food that they forgot to search and burn the farm.

Meanwhile I had made it safely to the barn, but when I opened the door, I realized that the forest was too far to reach without being seen. I looked around for somewhere else to hide. I saw the cabbage patch behind the barn. The leaves were huge so I figured I would hide under the leaves. I scurried into the cabbage patch and dropped onto my stomach to hide. A sudden shriek nearly frightened me to death. A woman, Monsieur Goulin's cousin, was already hiding there. She always wore a scarf over her head so I don't know if she had hair or not. She was extremely thin and when she spoke, she would always stare upward and make strange mumbling sounds.

She and I lay hidden in the cabbage leaves, praying for the German tanks to go. Finally, we heard the noisy engines start up and the German tanks drove away.

*   *   *

About three or four days later, we had our first sight of Americans! Three American tanks came through the field – just like the German tanks had come – and drove into the courtyard of the Goulin farm. Everyone was thrilled to see our liberators. Some of the girls started to run to kiss them, but the soldiers cautioned them to stay back. Monsieur and Madame Goulin approached the tanks to speak with them. They could not speak English and the Americans could not speak French. We watched them trying to communicate. The American soldiers had dirty faces and uniforms. When the people gave them fresh food from the farm, they were saying, "Thank you, thank you, thank you."

I remember thinking, "What are they saying? Why are they repeating that word?" I did not know one word of English then.

After the two American tanks left, the American army raised a single giant tent in a field on the adjacent farm[7]. It was just one tent, there were no smaller tents for the soldiers to

---

[7] The American 80th Infantry Division established its command post at Limey, France on September 4, 1944. Given the fact that its next command post moved to the town of Mamey on September 12th, it appears that the Americans used this command post for about one week. Based on this information, it is likely that Ida was liberated on September 3, 1944. The 80th Division used a "pyramidal" style tent for its command post when a house was unavailable for this purpose. The three tanks were likely from the 702nd Tank Battalion, which was attached to the 80th Division from August 1944 to March 1945. The 80th Division included three infantry regiments, the 317th, 318th and 319th. Combat continued to be fierce throughout this sector of France in the next few weeks. The Germans set up very strong defensive positions in the hills and ridges along the length of the Moselle River from Metz to Pont-a-Mousson to Nancy. Fighting at Pont-a-Mousson was especially ferocious with American forces capturing the famous Mousson hill with its ancient castle on September 14th, but then enduring major German counterattacks for the next three days. The city of Pont-a-Mousson was not in American control until September 19, 1944. Nancy, to the south, was liberated on September 16th, but Metz, to the north, was not captured until November 11th. As Ida recounts, the sounds of this intense fighting, called the "Battle of the Bloody Moselle," would have been constant and intense throughout this sector during the month of September 1944.

sleep in. The people from the Goulin farm liked to walk over to the big tent to see what the Americans were doing, but the soldiers did not let them get too close.

By this time, we were hearing the sounds of cannons, airplanes and bombing all around. Sometimes the bombs exploded nearby, but, thankfully, no shells landed on the farm. I remember listening to the cannon fire one day with Monsieur Goulin when the sound of artillery was not as close. Monsieur Goulin sighed with satisfaction and said, "Oh, they are further away," meaning that the American army was making progress and had driven the Germans farther east, away from the farm.

Nevertheless, even with the Germans gone and American soldiers on the farm, I was still skeptical of liberation. I don't know if it was true for the other people, but I was so downtrodden from seven months of fear and starvation that it was hard to believe that I was truly free. I remember saying to myself, "Let's see what happens." There had been other times when it looked as if I was safe – and I wasn't.

The warfare continued throughout our region of France during the next few weeks. As soon as she could, my mother acted to find and restore our family. We knew that Rosa was living in the city of Nancy (which was liberated on September 16th) and that Arnold was still hiding with the Herlin family in Pont-a-Mousson (which was liberated on September 19th). But we were very surprised to discover that my sister Eugenie was just one mile away from us! She had remained in hiding at the Touval farm since the time my family first escaped from the Gestapo in March 1944. If we had known, we could have visited each other.

At the first opportunity, probably in October 1944, my mother left to get Eugenie and the two of them returned directly to Pont-a-Mousson to retrieve Arnold. When they reached home, they found that our apartment house had been demolished by bombing. So they rented another apartment on *Place Duroc*, the town square of Pont-a-Mousson.

Meanwhile I remained behind at the Goulin farm. I was too weak from starvation to travel. I was not bedridden. I could walk, but I could do no labor. With my shrunken stomach, I still could not eat. It was even difficult to swallow. And without eating, I could not regain my health. Madame Goulin said to my mother, "Leave Ida here and we will get her eating again." It was sad to be separated again from *Maman*, but she knew I was in good care.

Madame Goulin had a plan. "I'm going to break an egg," Madame Goulin explained to her husband, "and put in one spoon of rum." Together they made me drink the rum and egg. The next day Madame Goulin mixed two eggs with two spoons of rum. The third day, three eggs and three spoons of rum. By the fourth day, I was tipsy from their treatment. My head was spinning as Madame Goulin turned to her husband and said, "I don't think this is such a good idea."

After that, they mixed cream with eggs and, little by little, I began to regain my strength. My recovery took many many weeks. I stayed at the Goulin farm until early January 1945. Then, one night, I was lying in bed and my sister Eugenie suddenly appeared in the doorway with a big smile. She came closer and said, "Ida, we have news that Papa may have survived the concentration camp."

I was thrilled. "Really?!"

Then my mother walked into my room. And who is standing behind my mother? Papa! I climbed from my bed to go to my father. His hair was shaven and his face was drawn. He was very quiet as he patted my head and I hugged him. And that was how I was reunited with my father after more than a year and a half.

I later learned that Papa had been liberated three weeks before we were. The Allies liberated Drancy concentration camp on August 17, 1944, followed one week later by the liberation of Paris on August 25th. Papa stayed in a Displaced Persons Camp, waiting for a chance to come look for us. But we were still in a war zone behind enemy lines. After we were liberated, my sister Rosa went to Paris and found Papa at the DP camp. Other than that, I know nothing of my father's ordeal in Drancy. He never spoke about it and refused any questions.

My parents and Eugenie stayed that night and left again the next day. I remained in recovery at the Goulin farm for yet another month. Finally, just before my sixteenth birthday in February 1945, I was able to return home to Pont-a-Mousson and rejoin my whole family – *Maman*, Papa, Rosa, Eugenie and Arnold. It was the best birthday present I ever received.

CHAPTER TEN

Aftermath and America

When I returned to Pont-a-Mousson to rejoin my family, they were living in a different apartment on *Place Duroc*, the main square. It was a white house that formed one of the stores along the arcade and had two apartments above the store. Our previous apartment building had been blown to bits. Everywhere that I looked, our lovely hometown was scarred with bomb craters, broken walls, and smashed out windows. The remains of the main bridge were still crumpled in the Moselle River. Still, the tall spires of the cathedral of Eglise Saint Martin remained standing on the opposite bank, undamaged, a symbol of recovery for the townspeople as they began to rebuild their lives.

I, too, was in shambles. Though I had been recovering for nearly five months at the Goulin farm, I remained extremely weak. I was like a hollow shell. The slightest effort exhausted me. I had no appetite and had to force myself to eat. I had no desire to go anywhere or do anything. I found pleasure in nothing. I lay in bed all day and all night. Even my love of piano had withered away. At night I was haunted by nightmares of being captured by the Gestapo and they would not let me go. In the day, I was gripped by a black trance that I could not escape.

What was wrong with me? I should have been happy. I was back home with my family and everyone had survived in good health. But I was miserable, and getting no better.

The winter of 1945 passed, and then the spring. I still did nothing but sleep and lie around the apartment. My family became accustomed to my depression as they resumed their lives. I know they cared about me, but after so many weeks without improvement, they did not know what to do to help me. They moved around me like an inanimate object in the room. I was stricken with a total physical and mental exhaustion. In hindsight, I believe the trauma of that nine and half months – the ceaseless fear and worry, the beatings and starvation, the repeated terrors that frightened me out of my wits – had taken everything out of me. It was just too much. If my ordeal had lasted another day or two longer, I honestly feel that I would have died. I had been terrified so much and so often, how much can a person take? I was just a child and yet I had had to fight for survival – every hour of every day for months – and do it completely alone.

When Passover came that spring, my parents invited two Jewish American soldiers to share in the traditional *Pesach seder*. The soldiers knew that we did not have much food so they brought bags full of food for the holiday meal. But *Maman* had scrounged up the ingredients for a tasty chicken soup. The soldier in the photograph would sometimes come to visit our home.

Ida (center) and her two sisters pose with one of the two Jewish American soldiers who helped them come to America. Notice the bomb damage to the city in the background, including the destroyed bridge and the spires of the Eglise Saint Martin cathedral.

The war ended in May 1945. Now it was the summer of 1945. I still struggled with physical and mental exhaustion, but I was determined to not let myself go. Ultimately, I knew I wanted to go to college and study music – but it seemed impossible. I could only walk for short distances and I had even lost my joy in music. How could I go to school in that condition?

As the hot days of June and July passed, I began to force myself to get up and play the piano. It took enormous effort and gave me no pleasure. At first, I could play very little before I was exhausted. But I pushed myself – little by little, more and more – until I could play the piano for an entire hour, then two, then three. I played without my former enthusiasm, but it became possible to imagine myself as a pianist again.

By August 1945, I felt strong enough to start piano lessons again. My former piano teacher, Mademoiselle Fariel, had stopped giving lessons after the war. But I learned of another young lady named Mademoiselle Passard, who had recently graduated from the *Conservatoire de Nancy* and was giving piano lessons. She lived nearby on the other side of *Place Duroc*. When I asked my father if I could resume lessons, I knew he would not say no. He was delighted. It was a sure sign that I was becoming myself again.

Meanwhile, Madame Pierre decided to return from Paris to Pont-a-Mousson with her boyfriend and her daughter. Since she owned our building, she had the authority to force us to leave our apartment and move to the smaller apartment on the top floor. I would have liked to have never seen her face again, but now, living above Madame Pierre, we would see her nearly every day. She had not changed. She expressed no remorse for her behavior during the war. She displayed the same arrogance.

In fact, no one ever talked about the abuses that had happened during the war, including my own family. No one, not even my mother, ever asked what had happened to me. No one knew how much I had gone through. Nor did I know what my family had suffered. What had happened to Papa when he was imprisoned at the concentration camp at Drancy? What had happened to my sisters and my mother? It was an undeclared zone of silence. No one talked about the war. No one asked. Even little Arnold, who was now eleven, asked and said nothing. All I knew was that the Herlins had become so fond of Arnold that they wished they could keep him after the liberation.

I am sure that my family felt it was best to forget the pain of the war and that it would be too upsetting to discuss it. I cannot know. But, looking back, it was not good for me because, in my weakness and depression, the silence made me feel like I was not worth anything. I felt that I deserved to be ignored and neglected. Keeping the secret of my trauma added to my sense of worthlessness. It was a very very difficult time for me, very difficult.

Ultimately, I was saved by my dearest old friend, my piano. I continued practicing through September 1945, building my hours and confidence, until I could resume lessons. I first went to Mademoiselle Passard, my new piano teacher, in October. We talked. I played Beethoven's *Appassionate Sonata*. She was expecting a beginner, so she was surprised at how well I could play. I said I wanted to go to the same *Conservatoire de Nancy* that she had just graduated from. She said that I was good enough – and that became my goal.

One day, after I had been taking piano lessons for about three months, I noticed my father's shoes on the floor. He always changed his shoes when he went to work. When I picked them up to put them in the closet, I dropped one. I discovered that it had a big hole in the sole, covered by a piece of cardboard. I was shocked to discover that both of Papa's shoes were worn through. I felt bad that he was walking with holes in his shoes, while I had the luxury of piano lessons.

I went to *Maman* with my discovery. "Well, you know, with your piano lessons every week, he doesn't have the money to re-sole his shoes."

That night, after my father came home, I went to him. "Papa, I saw your shoes today. I saw that you need soles. I don't have to take piano lessons."

"No, *mein kind* (my child)," he declared, "you are going to <u>continue</u> your piano lessons."

To gain admission to the *Conservatoire*, I first needed someone on the faculty to agree to be my piano teacher. In November 1945, I traveled to a professor's house in Laxou (the same suburb of Nancy where the Lion Lady lived) for my audition. It was crucial that I do well, so I was extremely nervous. The professor was grim from the very start. She sent me directly to the piano. I played a piece by Beethoven and a nocturne by Chopin. I thought I had performed well when I turned to face her.

"Who do you think you are?" she snarled, "Do you think that the Conservatory would accept you?! Never!"

In an instant, I was devastated. My life-long dream was crushed, my music career was over at age sixteen. I left her house in tears. I cried all the way to the railroad station. I cried on the train and was still crying when I arrived home. *Maman* listened to my sad news. "Don't cry, Ida. Maybe it is for the best. You will continue to study piano and you'll try another teacher."

Fortunately, there was one more way to get into the *Conservatoire de Nancy*. My piano teacher in Pont-a-Mousson still believed in me. "Did you know that they have a day at the Conservatory when anyone who does not have a teacher has a chance to audition?" she asked. "Then a jury decides if she is good enough to be admitted to the school. Do you want to do that?"

"Oh, yes," I replied. I wanted to get in so badly.

Two weeks later, I was sitting in a huge hall at the *Conservatoire de Nancy* with two grand pianos on the stage. The jury sat in the front row, composed of the head of the Conservatory, the Mayor of Nancy, and other dignitaries. And who is sitting at the side of the jury? The woman professor who said I wasn't good enough.

Then it was my turn. "Who is here to represent you?"

"No one," I answered.

I climbed onto the stage with my heart pounding. I played a nocturne and a beautiful exercise by Chopin. As soon as I finished, the Maestro, the head of the Conservatory, stood up and clapped! The others joined him in applause.

"Do you have a professor?" the Maestro asked.

"No," I said.

He turned to his left. "Well, Madame Minou, may I speak with you?"

The same professor, who had rejected me, faced him.

"Will you accept this young lady as your student?" he continued. The Maestro had no idea that she had thrown me out just two weeks before.

"Yes, I will," she answered, "if the young lady wants me as her professor?"

I said, "Yes." I was so green. I could have asked for another professor. So Madame Minou became my piano teacher for the next two years. She never changed her grim style. She was a very good teacher, but very strict and cold as ice. She never smiled. We never had a single conversation. I would walk in. I would play. She would correct me. Then I would leave. One hour each week. Not a word of praise, never ever.

It usually takes four years to finish a music degree at the Conservatory, but my family was planning to emigrate to America and I did not know how soon it would be. So I worked extra hard to finish before we left France. I was able to finish in two years. Like most serious pianists, I practiced eight hours a day, every day. I did not go to a movie, I did not date. On the days that I traveled to the Conservatory in Nancy, I would practice at night, which annoyed the neighbors, who sometimes called the police to complain.

Ida (left) and her sister Eugenie walking in Nancy in 1947.

I graduated in June 1948, sharing second prize in my class. The only time that I left my piano was when I served as a counselor at a summer camp for Jewish war orphans in 1947 and 1948. The camp was called "Verberie" and located just outside Paris. The children were all ages and had lost their parents during the war. We slept in tents. The experience reminded me of how extraordinarily lucky I was that my entire family had survived the Holocaust.

The plan to move to America first started in 1945, when my parents invited the two American soldiers to our house for Passover. Life is a wonder. It turned out that one soldier was from Philadelphia, where my father had a sister and brother, and one was from Cleveland, Ohio, where my mother had a brother. She also had a brother in Columbus, Ohio. The soldiers wrote to their wives, who then succeeded in contacting our relatives. We received letters from my uncles in Ohio and my aunt in Philadelphia. "After all the horrible years you have gone through there, why don't you come to America?" That gave us the idea.

The paperwork took a long time to complete. At last, in August 1948, we received permission to immigrate. First we had to go to the American Embassy in Paris to get our passports. Then we took a train to the port of Cannes on the Mediterranean. Our relatives in America generously paid for our Atlantic passage, $200 per person for our family of six[8]. The ship was a gigantic Polish passenger ship with a capacity of 1,154 passengers. The "Sobieski" was so big that we had to take a little boat to reach the place where it was anchored. Then we had to scale up the side – which is like climbing a tall cliff – on a scary, swaying rope ladder.

The passengers on board were from many countries, but mostly French. Some were Jewish and quite a few were Holocaust survivors from Poland. We had never been on a boat before. My parents and sisters were dreadfully seasick during the voyage, but my brother Arnold and I were fine. As passengers in Third Class, we were quartered in a dingy dormitory for about forty women and girls. The room lacked air and light and it was always noisy with people talking in the day and snoring at night. I tried to escape by spending as much time as possible on deck, enjoying the beautiful September weather.

I was more nervous than excited about coming to America. Here I was, 19 years old, born and raised in France, and suddenly I was on my way to a foreign country where I did not know one word of the language.

---

[8] Although Ida's father did not make much money in the United States, he secretly repaid them over the years.

Ida Hoffmann (center) socializes with some other passengers
on board the *Sobieski* enroute to America in September 1948.

Early in the trip, I was sitting on deck when the Captain of the Sobieski came and sat beside me. He was an Italian in his early 30's. He offered to show me around the ship and we made friends. He was an absolute gentleman. He took me to dinners and dancing in the First Class section, then he would walk me back down to our dorm in the Third Class section. He never tried to kiss me, but always shook my hand.

The voyage took eleven days with a brief stop in Canada on the way. We arrived at Ellis Island in New York City on September 21, 1948. I was overwhelmed by the crowds and commotion as my family twisted its way through the cattle chutes for many hours. We met my uncle and aunts and a few cousins at Ellis Island and then went straight to New Jersey, where we climbed into their two cars and set off for our new home in Philadelphia.

We stopped at a roadside diner on the way. This was my first taste of American life. I had never seen such a strange place, especially the long row of tall spinning stools along the counter. It made me dizzy to sit so high up on a seat that spun. I turned to my sister, who could speak some English and asked if we could sit at a table instead. She then asked my aunt, who said, "Of course you can."

"Tired" is the best way to describe how I felt in my new country. America was such a huge change. I could not read or understand English. I was exhausted from constant worrying, watchfulness and disorientation. I began to speak Yiddish for the first time because it was the only way that I could communicate with my American relatives. Before that, I understood Yiddish, but I could not speak it.

When we reached Philadelphia, we moved into my aunt's house on Diamond Street in the Wynnefield section, which was a Jewish neighborhood then. Their two sons went to stay with friends to make room for the six of us. My parents had one bedroom, my brother slept on the enclosed porch, and the three girls slept in one bed in another bedroom.

With the help of my aunt and uncle, my father quickly found work at a neighborhood factory that made paper boxes. Papa was short, but very strong, even now at age 58. It was his nature to be helpful, so when another worker could not lift something, Papa carried it for him. The other workers quickly took advantage of my father's kindness and began to give him all the heavy work. "Hey Pop, you do it." He stopped it after he realized what was happening.

After one month, we found our own apartment in Strawberry Mansion, another Jewish neighborhood in Philadelphia at that time. Although I could not speak English, relatives helped me get a job as a saleslady at a store on Germantown Avenue for $12 a week. The store sold nurses' uniforms and ladies underwear – and I somehow managed as I learned English.

Meanwhile, a young man, who lived in our neighborhood, heard that a family with three girls had moved in. He stopped my brother Arnold on the street and asked for the name of the youngest sister. Arnold said, "Ida" and gave him our telephone number. The man had not even seen me, but he called and asked me on a date. I would not go out with him, however, until I asked people in the neighborhood about him. "Oh, yes, Herman Firestone. His mother is a dressmaker. Oh yes, she's a very fine lady."

When I heard this, I figured it was safe to go out with Herman. Our first date was on my birthday in February 1949, though I did not tell him. At first, I was suspicious. He was an Air Force G.I., seven years older than I, working as a salesman in a shop. But we continued dating and he grew on me.

One year later, my family moved to another apartment on 31st Street in Strawberry Mansion above a grocery store near the park. Herman asked me to marry him – and I said yes. I also found a new job as a saleswoman at a hosiery store on Market Street in Center City Philadelphia, making $32.50 a week. Compared to $12 a week, I felt like a millionaire. Best of all, I now had enough money to buy a piano! I went to Jacobs Brothers and bought a piano for $350, which I paid in monthly installments. It felt wonderful to play piano again.

After a while, I had the idea that it would be nice to work in an office. I responded to a newspaper ad for Hartford Insurance Company at 4th and Chestnut. "Have you ever worked in an office?" the interviewer asked.

Of course, I had not, and I certainly had never seen anything like this gigantic office, which had about fifty desks in one huge room. "Yes," I lied.

"Where?" she asked.

"In France."

"Okay. Do you know what 'debit' and 'credit' mean?"

I had never heard such words before. "Oh, yes," I replied.

"Can you type?"

I figured that if I could play piano, I should also be able to type. "Yes," I said.

"Where did you type?" the interviewer asked.

"In France," I lied again.

She hired me! "Okay," she explained, "for now, you are going to do filing. But when one of our bookkeepers leaves, then you will take over her job." Then she showed me to my desk.

It was just my luck that a bookkeeper left after two months and I was expected to take her place. I had no idea what to do. I watched the girl in front of me. She was typing rapidly and her typewriter was flying back and forth. I tried to imitate her. I pushed all the buttons and nothing happened. A typewriter is nothing like a piano.

"Excuse me," I said to my coworker, "I think my typewriter is broken." I figured that you must have to turn a switch or something to turn the typewriter on.

"Oh," she said, "let me see." She sat at my typewriter and breezed through several lines. "I think it's okay."

But that was only half of my problem. "Excuse me, but what is 'debit' and 'credit'?"

She paused to look at me oddly, but then showed me how the debits go in one place and the credits go in another.

"Thank you," I said. I guess I must be smarter than I think because I learned to type and worked at Hartford Insurance for the next three years. I married Herman on July 8, 1951 and stopped working when I became pregnant with my son Craig in 1953.

CHAPTER ELEVEN

Piano, Painting and Public Speaking

In the summer of 1957, I was living in the Mt. Airy section of Philadelphia with my husband and son. My neighbor could often hear me playing piano because the windows were open. She had taken piano as a child and asked me to give lessons to her son. It worked out well. They recommended me to others and soon I had a small number of students. That was the beginning of my career as a piano teacher. More and more students came – until I had many students. I am still teaching piano today, over fifty years later.

In 1960, I discovered another new passion. I was painting our living room and the paint was sticking to my hands. When Herman and I went to Gimbel's Department Store to get some paint remover, I noticed a book on display with the extraordinary face of a Mongol man. I stared in wonder at the portrait, transfixed by the depth and the power of his amazing face. "Oh! What a face!" I exclaimed to Herman, "I would love to paint that face."

"What do you mean, 'paint that face'?" Herman asked. "You don't know how to paint!"

"I don't care. I want to paint that face." I had never painted in my life and yet I was instantly certain that I had to paint that face. I continued staring at the portrait.

"You can't just start painting faces," Herman advised. "You have to start simple – with cups and vases and fruit – before you can start painting faces!"

"I don't want to do that. I want to paint that face."

Herman shook his head in doubt.

"I'm buying the book," I declared.

"Go ahead, waste money."

I bought the book for a dollar. Then I bought an easel and some paints and started painting the Mongol's face. I loved painting. It flowed out of me as easily and naturally as music from my piano. Even I was astonished at how my brush could express and capture so much feeling. Where did it come from? I was always dreadful in drawing, yet now I could paint beautifully.

A week later, I gave a piano lesson to a student whose mother was an art teacher. She noticed the Mongol painting on my easel. "Oh, who is the artist?" she asked.

"I don't know if I'm an artist," I said, "but I painted it."

She moved closer to study the painting. "Well, you paint at the level of a third year college student."

"I do?!" I was shocked and thrilled. From the moment that I started that first painting I knew it was something that I wanted to pursue. I've been painting ever since.

*   *   *

In addition to piano and painting, the third passion in my life is public speaking about my Holocaust experience. It did not happen easily, nor was it planned, but I believe I was destined to do it. As I said before, there was a great silence in my family about what had happened during the war. In the aftermath of such ugliness and pain, we never asked about or spoke about our experiences. Like many Holocaust survivors, my personal story remained a secret – even with my own family. It is hard to explain, but after the war, nearly everyone wanted to forget the past and start life anew. I suppose that survivors felt that it would be too painful to remember what the Nazis had done to us and, for those who did not experience the Holocaust, it was too incredibly monstrous to comprehend.

So I lived with my secret for 35 years. I told my husband a little here and a little there, but no one else. That is why I was surprised one day in 1980 when the husband of a friend said, "Why don't you tell Ida about your group?" My friend was another Jewish French woman who came from Pont-a-Mousson. We had been friends for many years and we would get together occasionally to converse in French. Though we had grown up in the same hometown, we had never once talked about our experiences in France during the war.

My friend looked at her husband, who was a survivor from Poland, and then looked at me, a little embarrassed. "I don't know if you'll be interested. It's a group of Holocaust survivors."

"Are they French survivors?" I asked.

"No, from all over Europe. I can give you the telephone number if you think you want to join. In fact, the next meeting is at my house."

"Really?" I said. My friend was surprised when I said that I was so interested. I was instantly curious about the people in the survivors group. I wanted to know what happened to them and how they survived. Was it anything like what happened to me? I wanted to see what they looked like, how they acted, how they carried themselves. Since I'm a loner, I thought that these might be people with whom I could fit in.

A few weeks later, I went to the meeting at my friend's house. It was a large group of about twenty-five people, sitting in a circle in her living room. A spokeswoman explained that each person should say his or her name and whether he or she had survived a concentration camp or by hiding. One by one, each survivor spoke, but when it came to me, I immediately started to sob. I could not speak. The group waited quietly for me, but I could only cry, so they went on to the next person. For the rest of the night, I listened intently as other survivors told their stories of suffering and loss.

This was now 1980, thirty-five years after my ordeal. I was reliving the terrors of my past. I was overcome by powerful emotions that I had stuffed away since childhood. I did not know how to begin to express it. And the thought of telling my story in front of other people was terrifying to me. Still, I knew that I must.

Two months later, the survivors group had its next meeting. I tried again. The same thing happened. I could not speak, I could only cry.

Then another two months passed and I went to a third meeting. Once again, I could only cry. This happened five times in a row. Ten months had now passed and I had not yet even said my name in front of the group. But I was determined to try again.

Then, one day, I received a phone call from Stefanie Seltzer, the President of the group and a survivor herself. "Ida, I was supposed to go to a high school in Levittown today to speak, but my husband is very ill and I can't make it. Would you go there and speak about your experience?"

My heart stopped. "Oh no, I'm sorry Stefanie, but I can't, I just can't."

"Just think what good you can do for those students. They don't know about the Holocaust – and you will be teaching them something so important. At their age, this is something they should really know."

"I just can't..." I repeated.

"Please," she asked again.

I knew I could not do it for myself. But Stephanie was such a fabulous person and I admired her so much. I could not say no. "Alright," I said.

Now what would I do? I had never spoken about my Holocaust experience, not even to the survivor's group. Stephanie herself did not know my story. Nor had I ever done any public speaking before. I was very nervous as I drove to the high school and a teacher brought me to a classroom with about thirty-five students. I intended to speak, but emotions overwhelmed me. I cried. Then I tried again. I continued to cry, unable to speak. I cried for maybe ten minutes as the students sat quietly and waited. Eventually I forced myself to begin.

It was very difficult, but I finally told my story. The students stood up. They clapped. They came over and kissed me! I could not have received a better response.

I knew then that this would be my mission – to teach the next generation about the Holocaust and tolerance. At the next meeting of the survivors group, I told my story. The Jewish Community Relations Council added me to their Holocaust Speakers Bureau. I spoke at many schools to many students. For the first two years, I would cry every time that I told my story, but I became more comfortable. I have been talking to students ever since.

One time, about six years ago, I spoke before a large auditorium with five hundred students. When I had finished, a young lady asked me a question. "After what happened to you during the war, can you trust anyone? Do you trust your friends?"

I don't like to tell people that I am a loner because they might think there is something wrong with me. But I cannot lie. I have to be honest with the students. "Well," I confided to her – privately, in front of 500 people! – "I have friends, but no close friends."

"Oh. Does it bother you?" she asked.

"Not really," I said.

The same student later wrote me a letter and said, "I feel sorry for you that you don't have any close friends. I couldn't live without my close friends."

I thought deeply about her words. Now it did bother me to lack close friends. How badly had the war affected me that I did not dare to trust people? When I was in hiding from the Gestapo, I had to be on guard at all times. To survive, I learned that I could trust no one. If someone discovered that I was a Jew, I could be sent to a death camp. If someone asked me a question, even an ordinary question, I had to be careful about my every word. I might accidentally reveal something that could cost me my life. Survival required distrust.

Though the war had ended almost sixty years ago, I realized that I was still guarded. My trauma had trained me against trusting people. I thought about my sisters and my brother. They all have many friends and often talk about their close friends. I felt bad that I seemed so different. Other than my immediate family, whom I love dearly, I did not have any close friends.

That is the tragedy of my experience, but maybe also its message. The fear, distrust and hatred that comes from racism is a terrible terrible thing. Some of the Germans were good people. They were not all Hitlerians. We cannot condemn people by their religion, or race, or country, or group. We are all human beings and we must treat everyone respectfully as *menschen*, as fellow human beings.

When I look back on the Holocaust, especially when I see genocide happening in other places today, I am sad and wonder why. But I do not lose hope. I tell my story to the next generation so that they, too, will not lose hope. Yes, I nearly perished at the hands of hate and bigotry, but I also survived because of the kindness and courage of many strangers. We must trust in the basic goodness in people, that we are all children of the same God. We cannot allow fear, hate, and prejudice to destroy our capacity for tolerance, respect, and understanding – for people of all kinds.

When I was in hiding from the Nazis, I held onto hope by writing poems. I had never written poems before and, after liberation, I never wrote poems again. Still, during those dreadful nine months, my poems were as crucial to my survival as food itself. They surrounded me with spiritual protection even as the hidden pins that held them were pricking my flesh. I had written about forty poems in all, pouring my fears and feelings into them. But after we came to America, I was heart-broken to discover that my precious poems had been lost! I felt like I had lost a part of myself. But what could I do? They were gone forever.

Then, about three years ago, I was preparing a recital for my piano students. One of my teenagers did not know what she wanted to play. I said, "Would you like to play something from Bach?"

"Maybe."

"I once played a Prelude and a Fugue from Bach at my recital in France," I said. "I bet you would like it."

"Oh yes!" she exclaimed, "if you played it, then I want to play it."

I had to go hunting for my old sheet music to find the piece. And there, pressed safely inside the Bach music, were all of my original poems, written on the scraps of paper I had pinned inside my clothes in 1944.

Sixty years later, I was whole again.

EPILOGUE

Ida's father, Adolphe Hoffmann, died of a heart attack in February 1973 at the age of 83. Her mother, Berthe Hoffmann, "my best friend," died in Philadelphia in 1964 at the age of 71 from congestive heart failure.

Ida's oldest sister Rosa now lives in Silver Springs, Maryland. She has three children and two grandchildren. Her other sister, Eugenie, lives in White Plains, New York with her husband. She has four children and five grandchildren. Her brother Arnold, now known as Charles, is a retired chef living in the Philadelphia area. He has three children and four grandchildren.

Today Ida Hoffmann Firestone lives with her husband Herman in Philadelphia. She continues teaching piano, painting, and public speaking about the Holocaust. She has one son, Craig, and two grandchildren.

Ida's mother, Berthe Hoffmann, in 1957.

AUTHOR'S COMMENTS

I had no idea that Ida was a painter until I entered her house to conduct our first interview. Marvelous paintings commanded every wall of her Philadelphia home. I did not know it yet, but I had just stepped into France in World War II. I was already seeing images from Ida's childhood experience of the Holocaust.

The first painting to catch my eye was the one chosen for the cover of this book, my personal favorite, a Monet-like meadow bursting with sunlight and joy. More paintings filled Ida's living room with lovely large images of French towns and countryside — idyllic scenes of Pont-a-Mousson, Strasbourg, Meurthe/Moselle, and Ida's father.

As we worked on the book in the months that followed, I learned the details behind each painting, nearly every one painted from memory. As I listened to Ida, I often gazed at these paintings. There was such beauty and serenity in these paintings, yet they represented terror, anxiety and loneliness. The contrast is characteristic of Ida — a sweet, very likeable person who lacks close friends; a humble, soft-spoken woman with the iron will of a Napoleon. It is a contrast that was forged in 1944 when a simple Jewish girl had to somehow maintain an outward image of calm normality, while she churned inside with fear and the pangs of starvation. I came to see Ida's paintings as the outside image of hope and her poems as the inside turmoil of reality. Her paintings depicted how life should be, while her childhood poems cried of how life should never be.

My hope is to have woven Ida's paintings and poems with her words and memories to bring the reader into that unforgettable time and place in history — through the eyes and tears of one extraordinary young girl.

This book marks my second effort to capture the complete stories of Holocaust survivors and save them for posterity. It is not enough to record the testimony of atrocities and suffering. If we are to fully comprehend the loss of humanity, it is important to also see these families before the great destruction. We need to know details of what life was like for victims like little Ida Hoffmann before the war and also what life was like after the war as they tried to rebuild their shattered lives. Only by knowing their entire story, can we begin to realize the magnitude of the tragedy and loss.

One exhibition at the United States Holocaust Memorial Museum is "The Tower of Faces." It is a three-story display of hundreds of pre-war photographs of ordinary Jews living in the town of Eisiskes in Lithuania. Its purpose is to remember the victims of the Holocaust as simple ordinary people — by viewing photographs of their individual smiles and festivities — rather than nameless skeletons for the crematorium. Similarly, in my own small way, I hope to convey the entire stories of witnesses like Ida Hoffmann Firestone, who were destined to survive the Holocaust and are still alive to tell their essential stories.

I was also destined – to meet Ida. By coincidence, I was seated beside her at a B'nai Brith luncheon in northeast Philadelphia, where Ida had finished telling her story of survival. I was immediately taken by the exquisite manners and grace of this tiny woman with such enormous courage. I explained that I was there at the invitation of another member, who is also a Holocaust survivor. As we ate our lunch, I explained that I had just completed writing the memoir for this woman (which was published in 2005 and is also available from Xlibris). Ida said that she too wished that someone would write her story someday. "I will write your story," I volunteered immediately, "it would be my privilege."

Ida blessed me with that rare privilege, which I have done my best to honor.

TIMELINE OF HISTORICAL EVENTS

This timeline recreates key dates and events of the period in which Ida was fleeing and hiding from the Nazis in 1944. Some dates are estimated using dates that are certain. A few historical events are also noted to provide a broader historical context for Ida's story.

DATE IN 1944	EVENTS
March 1 (Wed.)	German soldiers come to arrest Ida's family at home at 5AM. The bakers hide them.
March 2 (Thurs.)	Ida and Rosa hide at friend's house in Pont-a-Mousson for the night, then leave in morning.
March 2 (Thurs.)	Ida and Rosa take night train to Paris; arrive early in the morning on Friday, March 3.
March 3 (Fri.)	Ida and Rosa go to Madame Pierre's café in the morning; hide in a brothel hotel for the night.
March 4 (Sat.)	Ida and Rosa go to Drancy concentration camp to see their father, who sends then back to Paris to Madame Charon.
March 4 to 8	Ida and Rosa stay with Madame Charon for several days.
March 9 (Thurs.)	Ida and Rosa move to stay one night with "crazy" woman, who was talking to England on the radio.
March 10 (Fri.)	Ida and Rosa stay with the "dirty-house" woman who recommends prostitution. Rosa gets a job in Paris. Ida decides to return to Pont-a-Mousson.
March 11 (Sat.)	Ida is saved by a total stranger on the train who tells the authorities that she is his niece.
March 12 (Sun.)	Ida arrives in Pont-a-Mousson at 5AM. She avoids a collaborator and is hidden for the day by Monsieur Poincare.
March 12 (Sun.) to April 2 (Sun.)	Monsieur Louire hides Ida in flour sack and drives her to the Touval farm, where she reunites with her mother and sister Eugenie for 3 weeks.
April 2 (Sun.)	Ida is sent to live with the Lion Lady in Laxou for the next 3 months.
April 6 (Thurs.)	Nazis arrest 51 people at a French home for children at Izieu. All are sent to Drancy for deportation to Auschwitz. Only one survives.

June 6 (Tues.)	D-Day: the Allied armies land in Normandy.
June 10 (Sat.)	The Nazis murder every citizen in the French town of Oradour-sur-Glane.
June 24 (Sat.)	When the Lion Lady goes on vacation, Ida is sent to another farm. Ida is asked to leave after three days for fear of being caught harboring a Jew.
June 27-28 (Wed. - Thurs.)	Ida wanders to the farm of an older couple. She stays in the stable for two days, then flees to escape a bounty on hidden Jews.
June 29 (Thurs.)	Ida hides in the woods for a night, a day, and another night.
June 30 (Fri.)	Ida wanders and finds shelter with a kind giant woman for four days until her son is caught spying under the bed.
July 5 (Wed.)	Ida wanders to a farm where she stays two days and then accompanies the couple to church on Sunday.
July 9 (Sun.)	Ida flees discovery as a Jew and spends two more days hiding in the woods.
July 11 (Tues.)	Ida rides the bus back to the Lion Lady's house and spends another two weeks.
July 18 (Tues.)	Ida is surprised to find her sister Rosa is now living in Nancy.
August 2 (Wed.)	Ida makes a phone call to her mother and is caught by the Gestapo.
August 3 (Thurs.)	Ida goes to say goodbye to Rosa and spends the night in Rosa's room at the pension in Nancy.
August 4 (Fri.)	Ida and Rosa go to the Gestapo as ordered and narrowly escape capture because of a French spy.
August 4 (Fri.)	Ida goes to the Nancy train station, then to a Russian collaborator's café, then to a brewery in Champigneuelle.
August 4 (Fri.)	Anne Frank and her family are arrested by the Gestapo in Amsterdam, Holland.
August 5-6 (weekend)	Ida spends two days and nights hiding in unlocked apartments in Nancy.
August 7 (Mon.)	Ida returns to the brewery to be secretly transported to the Goulin farm in Limey, where she is reunited with her mother.
August 17 (Thurs.)	The Drancy Concentration Camp is liberated, including Ida's father.
August 21 (Mon.)	Ida develops a severe toothache two weeks after arriving at the farm.
August 25 (Fri.)	Paris is liberated by Allied forces.
August 31 (Fri.)	German tanks arrive to burn the Goulin farm.
Sept. 3 (Sun.)	American tanks arrive to liberate Ida and her mother at the Goulin farm.